PROFIT PLANNING AND CONTROL IN PUBLIC ENTERPRISES IN INDIA

PROFIT PLANNING AND CONTROL IN PUBLIC ENTERPRISES IN INDIA

B.B. LAL

ATLANTIC PUBLISHERS AND DISTRIBUTORS

Published by
ATLANTIC PUBLISHERS AND DISTRIBUTORS
B-2, Vishal Enclave, Opp. Rajouri Garden, New Delhi-27
Phones : 5413460, 5429987
e-mail : info@atlantibooks.com

Sales Office
4215/1, Ansari Road, Darya Ganj, New Delhi-110 002
Phones : 3273880, 3285873, 3280451
Fax : 91-11-3285873
web : www.atlanticbooks.com

ISBN 81-7156-919-6

Typeset at
APD Computer Graphics, Delhi

Printed in India at
Mehra Offset Press, Delhi

ACKNOWLEDGEMENTS

At the very outset I acknowledge my indebtedness to my parents and teachers but for whom I would not have been able to write even this acknowledgement. I am particularly grateful to Dr. B.P. Agrawal for his valuable guidance and meaningful discussions, and to Dr. A.N. Choubey for his invaluable comments at the various stages of this work.

I owe my gratefulness to Dr. Shrawan Kumar Goswami for being a constant source of inspiration and to Dr. V.K. Sinha for taking pains in going through the final draft.

I am glad to acknowledge the help and cooperation extended to me by the authorities and officials of BSL Bokaro, ITI, TSL, BPCL, Naini (Allahabad), MECON, CCL, HEC, Ranchi and the library-staff of MTI (SAIL), BSL, IIPA and Marwari College, Ranchi. My sincere and heartfelt thanks are due to all my friends and well wishers for their selfless cooperation and to Amar Nath, my favourite student, for providing assistance in compilation of the work.

I must not miss to count the affection and hospitality extended to me by my father-in-law, Sri G. Dass, Maurjpur Delhi, my friend, Mr. N.C. Srivastava, Allahabad during the course of collection of necessary information.

Last but not the least, I can never forget to appreciate the overwhelming support provided by my wife Pushpa and my sons, Nikhil and Vipul.

B.B. LAL

INTRODUCTION

Direct participation of the Government in the field of business and industry was one of the most important decisions of the Government of independent India. The Industrial Policy Resolutions 1948 and 1956 show the determination of the Government to take forward the country on a socialistic pattern through the policy of mixed economy. To fulfil this goal, the Government of India established a number of enterprises covering a vast field under the public sector. Though this sector performed well in regard to employment generation, so far as the financial outcome is concerned, it was not achieved upto the expectations of the country even after a long gap of its birth. Hence, there has been a big hue and cry over the policies adopted earlier regarding this sector.

The Estimates Committee, the Committee on Public Undertakings of Lok Sabha and the Administrative Reforms Commission were constituted and appointed by the Government with an objective to take stock of the workings of Public Sector and to improve its functioning. The Committees and the Commission observed clearly that the failure of this sector in regard to resource generation was mainly due to the lack of strict financial management and control. So the Administrative Reforms Commission categorically mentioned that there was an earnest need to strictly implement the financial planning and control system. The Administrative Reforms Commission observed.... "An effective mechanism of financial management and control can be built up only on a sound budgetary system. The budget of a public enterprise has not only to serve the requirements of external accountability and internal control but it has also to provide a plan of action, a framework in which to review progress and standard against which to review performance."[1]

This clearly shows the importance of profit planning and control (budgeting) to improve the functioning of an enterprise. Thus, whether the Indian public sector undertakings are adopting the budgeting, a key to productive financial planning and control in its true spirit, becomes a subject of study. Therefore, an attempt has been made here to probe the matter.

The study incorporates both the conceptual framework of the profit planning and control as well as its empirical study. Under the empirical study, it includes the study of some selected Indian public sector undertakings with respect to the practical application of the profit planning and control adopted by these units.

The public sector in India is a vast field comprising the constituents of manifolds. Therefore, it was not practically possible to incorporate all the undertakings in the study. Keeping this in view, the steel sector, a giant in public sector and mother industry for all infrastructural development of the nation, has been considered for the study. Further to make an indepth study, the Bokaro Steel Plant (BSL) has been taken as a model unit of the steel sector. However, to substantiate the study, some selected units from all important sectors, have been surveyed and budgetary practices adopted by these undertakings have been looked into briefly. The book has been shaped into eight chapters as briefed below :

Chapter one is related to the policies adopted mainly after Independence regarding the growth of public sector undertakings in India. The chapter further throws light upon the controversies arisen over the very existence of the public sector or its restructuring. Apart from this, it also covers the reformative measures taken by the government under its new Industrial Policy, 1991, that brought about a fundamental change in the policies adopted earlier for this sector.

The second chapter deals with the conceptual framework

1. Administrative Reforms Commission Report — *Public Sector Undertaking*, 1967, p. 56.

of budgets and budgetary exercises. It also explicits the importance of budgeting as an effective tool of management accounting. It makes it clear that it is he, 'who plans his work and works his plan', gets success.

Chapter three presents the classification of budgets on various lines. It also covers the process of preparation of a revenue budget in all its facets, *i.e.,* sales budget, production budget, raw materials budget, production overheads budget, manpower budget, administrative expenses budget and cash plan in an elaborated form.

Chapter four studies the budgeting-process regarding capital investment proposals with a tune to its return during its life period. It explicitly explains all important techniques being used in appraising the capital investments-proposals.

Chapter five incorporates some important observations made by Estimates Committee, Committee on Public Undertakings and Administrative Reforms Commission on budgetary practices with respect to the Indian public sector undertakings from time to time.

Chapter six deals with the process of budgeting adopted by public sector undertakings in India. For this purpose, six undertakings, representing various sectors, *i.e.,* communication, service, jobbing, energy and heavy industries, have been undertaken. It encompasses a brief analysis of the methodology adopted by the selected units in regard to the preparation of revenue and capital budgets. But for a detailed analysis, a thorough look has been cast upon the steel sector discussed separately in the succeeding chapter with a view to presenting a comprehensive picture of the study.

Chapter seven makes an indepth study of the budgeting adopted by the public sector steel industry with special reference to the Bokaro Steel Plant (BSL). An effort has been made to frame this chapter in a comprehensive form with the inclusion of all three important aspects of a budgetary exercise *i.e.*, budgeting-techniques, planning, programming and lastly the controlling of the planned activities. The chapter makes a detailed discussion about the budgetary provisions, their nature, and types along with the co-ordinating agencies involved in the process. Under the planning and programming aspect, it makes a thorough study of the budgeting-process *i.e.,* the initiation of budget proposals, discussions, finalisation and approval. The budgeting for capital expenditures — planned and non-planned, has also been dealt with separately. Further, the most important aspect of the budgeting *i.e.,* controlling aspect has been visualized and analysed in detail with respect to all key points *i.e.,* costs, volume, expenditures, usage, price, sensitivity analysis and techno-economic variances.

The last chapter presents a summary of the whole body of the study. Besides, it includes the conclusions drawn with respect to the hypothesis of the work along with some important suggestions followed by appendix and bibliography.

The author hopes that this work will certainly be fruitful in framing policies to improve the functioning of public sector undertakings in India through strict adherence to the profit planning and control with a view to running the public sector on business lines and will serve as a reference for the students of financial management.

CONTENTS

1

Public Sector at Cross Roads

Rationale of the Public Sector

In the last few decades, the State has emerged as an active participant in the economic affairs of a country. In most of the countries, the Government is actively and directly involved in managing the economic and industrial activities, "These activities range from transport system — railways, road, air and shipping enterprises and waterways — the generation of power and its distribution, irrigation with vast network; the mining and processing of coal, iron and other minerals; banking and insurance — to industrial establishment of all kinds, such as integrated steel plants, machine tools, fertilisers and chemicals, the manufacture of aircraft, of locomotives and of industrial and commercial activity."[1] Thus, there is hardly any sphere of human activity which is not controlled and regulated by the State.

The need for public enterprise arises out of the fundamental duty of the State to work for the welfare of the people. "There are certain vital things which the individual can never do, either because he has not the necessary strength to perform them or because they would not pay him. The State is the only entrepreneur who can undertake such task."[2] Public enterprises are promoted for equitable distribution of social products which forms the very basis of the general welfare of the society.

---

1. Khera, S.S., *Government in Business*, National Publishing House, New Delhi, 1963, p. 7.
2. Dr. Agrawal, R.C., *State Enterprises in India*, Chaitanya Publishing House, Allahabad, 1961, p. 7.

The main object of the public sector is to ensure a balanced economic growth of the entire country and to lay down the foundation for the building up of a super — structure. Besides the basic and key industries, public sector enters into diverse fields such as promotional and credit institutions, transport organisations, trading agencies among others — all directed to accelerating economic growth, curbing monopoly and concentrating economic power in few hands, releasing the country from the burden of dependence on others and making it more and more self-reliant and, above all, bring the benefits of growth to the weaker and neglected sectors of the community and economy as a whole.[3] Apart from this, the public sector assists in the creation of employment opportunities, earning and saving of foreign exchanges by means of export and import substitution; promotion of research and development activities to eliminate the dependence on foreign technologies.

The government has to keep in view the long-term strategy for the sound economic growth. With this view, most of the countries have introduced planning to accelerate economic growth. For successfully implementing a plan, mere regulation and control of economy is not enough, but the active participation of the state in economic and industrial fields is inevitable, irresistible and compulsive. As Mr. Hanson states that the "Public enterprise without a plan can achieve something, a plan without public enterprise is likely to remain on paper."[4] Thus, the objective of planned economies cannot be fulfilled without direct participation of Government in business and industry. The public sector plays an important role in accelerating the economic growth of developing countries whose national economy is operated according to a plan.

In a country like India, where the industrial base had not been built up sufficiently till independence, the need for building up the industrial base by active participation of the state becomes imperative. After independence, the first Government of free

3. *Yojana*, Sept. 15, 1973, Vol. 16, p. 657

4. Hanson, H.H., *Public Enterprise and Economic Development*, Routledge and Kegan Paul, London, 1959, p. 183.

India under the leadership of Prime Minister Pandit Jawaharlal Nehru had decided to take forward (accelerate) the Indian economy under the definite plans.

The Planning Commission in India has emphasised the role of public sector as a prime mover in the process of economic development. "The public sector has to expand rapidly. It has not only to initiate developments which the private sector is either unwilling or unable to undertake, it has to play the dominant role in shaping the entire pattern of investments in the economy whether it makes the investments directly or whether these are made by the private sectors."[5] The Government of India, after independence, has come forward to establish the industrial base and has established basic industries as power, coal, oil, fertilisers, atomic energy, iron and steel, machine tools, heavy machinery, heavy chemicals, transport, communication and strategic industries, etc.

Smt. Indira Gandhi, the former Prime Minister of India had strongly advocated the rationality of public sector in these words.... "We advocate public sector for three reasons: to gain control of the commanding heights of the economy, to promote critical development in terms of social gain or strategic value rather than primarily on profit- and to provide commercial surpluses with which to finance further economic development."[6]

Thus, the task of the public sector is to harmonize the plans and operations of their enterprise and dovetale them with larger national goals that would directly promote the economic well-being of the community. Till seventies, the government gave more and more stress upon the physical development without giving much importance to the profit earned by this sector. The public sector was established as a mirror of socialist pattern of society. the guiding factor of international relations. Later on during eighties the government started to re-think over its policies because of recurring losses incurred by most of the units of public enterprises since their inception. Accordingly, the fundamental changes brought up in nineties regarding the policies adopted

5. Govt. of India, *Planning Commission*, 2nd Five Year Plan, p. 22.

6. *A hand Book of Information on Public Enterprises*, 1970, p. IX.

earlier. Today we find a sea change not only in India but in many other developing countries of the world in their economic policies. The people, who only a few years back swore by the public sector and thought them to be the panacea for the removal of poverty, are thinking twice before justifying the existence of public enterprises. These are the days of liberalisation, privatisation, and globalisation. The dawn of a new competitive society is on the horizon. To understand this unique phenomenon, it is essential to know, what went wrong with the public sector enterprises after all?

Evolution of Public Sector Undertakings in India : A Brief Review

Though the history of state intervention and participation in India can be traced back to the Mauryan period and some evidence of its existence during the Mughal period are there, but the real impetus influenced by some ideology for the growth of public sector came only after independence. The British rulers, in order to meet some temporary exigencies resorted to the establishment of public sector but by and large it was a period of free economy dictated by British interest. Keeping in view, a special emphasis has been given only on the policies adopted regarding the growth of public sector on post-independence period.

In ancient India, state interference in economic life existed basically in two forms — the state assistance to the industries and regulation of these industries by the state. "In Gautam Buddha period, the regulation of prices and costs came as a natural sequel to the ideals of co-operation on which Indian society...... was based."[7] During the Mauryan Age, India gave to the world the first taste of 'State Socialism' and Chandragupta Maurya was the first to establish a state of modern type. and organised the administration on rational basis with the assistance of his able Minister Kautilya.[8] At that time various kinds of public enterprises like mining, salt, fishing, forestry, and irrigation

---

7. Dass, S. Kumar, *The Economic History of India*, 1944, pp. 177-78.

8. Sharma, T.R., *Working of State Enterprises in India*, p. 1.

existed. All these were run under the control and supervision of various affairs incharge, such as 'Lavanadhyaksha' (responsible for manufacture of salt, meeting public demand and fixing the price), Akaradhyaksha (incharge of mining), 'Lohadhyaksha' (incharge of bare metal manufacture), Laksandhyaksha' and the 'Rupadhyaksha' (incharge of currency), 'Swarnadhyaksha' (gold extraction) and the 'Khandhyaksha' (sea mines).[9]

In the medieval period state workshops were the important segments of Indian economy. During this, India was under the control of Mughal emperors. The Mughal Sultans took a great interest in maintaining state Karkhanas at different places such as Lahore, Agra, Fatehpur, Ahmedabad, and Kashmir.[10] In the medieval period, mining also came in the ambit of state activity. A large number of Karkhanas, Royal workshops were attached to the imperial households.[11] There were 36 units of state enterprises during the period of firoz Shah which comes up to more than one hundred during the regime of Akbar the great.

The Britishers came to India as traders but later on they became the ruler of this country. They adopted such policies that were helpful to exploit the Indian market that could serve the best interest of their own country. The approach of the British Government in India to economic matters continued to be that of *Lessez faire* which transformed the country into a colonial appendage of the British Empire.

The administrative need of the British Government in India compelled them to re-think over the policies adopted till 1825. By then they had realised this fact that without considering the economic growth of India, they could not rule over it for a long time. Resulting which the 'Indian Postal System' in 1837, Indian Railway in 1853, and Geological Survey of India in 1870 were some of the important State Undertakings established by the British rulers in India during the nineteenth century. Later on the First World War proved an eye opener for the Britishers. Only

9. Prakash, Om, *The Theory and working of State Corporation with special reference to India*, 1962, p. 51.
10. Sarkar, Jadunath, *Mughal Administration*, 1935, p. 189, quoted by Sharma, T.R., p. 1.
11. *Lok Udyog*, July, 1970, p. 441. Para 3 Public Enterprises in Medieval India.

after this, they paid a special attention towards the establishment of some selected industries by the State.

"In 1916, Indian Industrial Commission was set up under the Chairmanship of Sir Thomas Holland."[12] The commission was instructed to examine and report upon the possibilities of future industrial development in India and to submit recommendations for a permanent policy of industrial stimulation.[13] The Commission submitted its report in 1918 in which a change in the industrial policy was strongly advocated.

In 1921, the Government accepted the recommendations of AG Worth Committee, that the lines owned by the State were to be run by it. In fact it was the first significant move in the direction of State participation in the economic activities during the British rule. National Planning Committee was set up under the chairmanship of Pandit Jawaharlal Nehru to prepare a comprehensive scheme of national planning. The committee stressed the need for the regulation and control of economic activities by the state.

To meet the necessities raised during the Second World War, the government began increasingly to recognise the need of helping industrialisation in the country through a state participation. In 1944 the Bombay Plan was prepared by eight prominent industrialists of the country. The planners admitted the role of the state in planning the national economy. "It is inevitable that in executing a comprehensive Plan of Economic Development, the State should exercise in the interest of community, a considerable measure of intervention and control."[14] Besides, a statement on the Industrial policy was made by Lord Wavele on April 21, 1945. It was the first statement of the government in favour of the principle of mixed economy.[15]

An Advisory Planning Board was set up by the Government under the chairmanship of Mr. K.C. Neogy, in October, 1946. The Advisory Board recommended that apart from Defence

12. Austey, Vera, *The Economic Development of India*, 1941, p. 216.

13. Lord Hardinage quoted by Desai, A.R., *Social Background*, p. 90.

14. Quoted by Nag, O.S., *A Study of Economic Plans for India*, 1949, p. 17.

15. Ignacy Sachs, *Pattern of Public Sector in Underdeveloped Countries*, p. 14.

Industries and any industry or branch of any industry which it might be found desirable to start as a state enterprise due to reluctance of private capital to undertake it, the nationalisation of the following should be considered : coal, minerals, oil, iron steel, motor, air and river transport.[16] Some other important landmarks of the public sector during the British regime in India are radio telephone service between India and England in 1939, the nationalisation of private owned Hindustan Aircraft in 1942, the nationalisation of the telephone system in Calcutta, Madras and Bombay in 1943, the nationalisation of railway in 1944, and the nationalisation of the Overseas Telecommunication Service in 1947.[17]

Thus, before independence, the scope of the state enterprise in the industrial field was confined to some basic industries that were influenced by the British interest mainly. But the more important factor was that whatever achievements were made in this field were the result of an administrative need and public awareness.

Policy Framework and Growth : After Independence

After Independence the country had to embark on a plan which could ensure a rapid economic growth. This began in the shadow of the British Raj in India which was also influenced by the socialist thought and Indian value system. Instead of the two extremes of centrally controlled economy on the model of the then Soviet Russia (U.S.S.R.) and the free society of the U.S.A., India chose a middle path for its economic development. Thus the philosophy of mixed economy was accepted as the guiding principle in matters of economic policies. This ideological inclination necessitated the growth of public sector in India. It was thought that the state has to perform not only its traditional functions, but also to actively participate in the industrialisation of the country and establish its own enterprises. In this regard, the government announced its policy statements from time to time. These policy statements also explicit the growth of public sector after independence. "The history of public enterprises in India since

16. Quoted by P. Prasad, *Problems of Public Enterprises in India*, p. 95.

17. Khera, S.S., *Government in Business*, Asia Publishing House, 1963. p. 54

Independence may be traced through the several Industrial Policy statements made by the Government."[18] In the light of priorities and plan, chalked out by the government, the first Industrial Policy of independent India was announced by the Govt. in April, 1948. The policy gave a concrete shape to the concept of mixed economy and paved the way for the establishment of public sector enterprises in India. In the meantime, "The public sector was born out of the urge expressed by Pandit Jawaharlal Nehru as early as 1948 when he said that the state must be more and more the organiser of constructive industry and again that according to our thinking the strategic points of economic development should be controlled by the state or by the planning apparatus."[19]

Industrial Policy 1948

Dr. S.P. Mukherjee, the then Minister for Industries announced the first Industrial Policy of India on April, 1948. The policy statement said : "The problem of state participation in Industry and the condition in which private enterprise should be allowed to operate must be judged."[20] The industrial policy resolution contemplated a mixed economy, reserving a sphere for the private sector and another for public sector. The industries were divided into the following four broad categories :

(a) The policy laid down that the manufacture of arms and ammunition, the production and control of atomic energy and the ownership and management of railway transport should be the exclusive monopoly of the Central Government and in emergency, the government could take over any other industry vital for national defence.

(b) The basic and key industries like coal, iron & steel, aircraft manufacture, ship building, mineral ores and manufacture of telephone and telegraphic and wireless apparatus excluding radio receiving sets are included.

18. Khera, S.S., *Government in Business*, National Publishing House, New Delhi, 1977, p. 15.

19. Yojana, Editorial, Public Sector Parameters of Performance, September 1973, p. 657.

20. *Government of India Resolution on Industrial Policy*, April 6, 1948.

Existing units of these industries remain in the private sector but the state....will be exclusively responsible for new undertakings except where in the national interest, the state itself finds it necessary to secure the cooperation of private enterprise subject to such control and regulations as the Central Government may prescribe.[21] In this regard, the government also made its stand clear that up to ten years, it would not interfere and the case of nationalisation of such industries would be examined only after ten years. In case of acquiring any industry in the national interest, the government also made it clear that "when such acquisition will take place, the fundamental rights guaranteed under the constitution will be observed and compensation will be awarded on a fair and equitable basis."[22]

(c) In this category, eighteen basic and key industries of vital importance of national interest were included. These were the salt, automobiles, tractors, prime movers, electric engineering, heavy machinery, machine tools, heavy chemicals, fertilisers, pharmaceuticals and drugs, electrochemical industries, non-ferrous metals, rubber manufacture, power and industrial alcohol, cotton and woollen, textiles, cement, sugar, paper and newsprint, air and sea transport, minerals and industries related to defence. It was decided that these industries would operate in the private sector subject to the regulations, control and direction of the government.

(d) All the other industries that were not included in the above categories, were left for the private sector (individual as well as co-operative). It was further stated that the state would also progressively participate in this field and would not hesitate to intervene whenever the progress of an industry is unsatisfactory under the private enterprise.[23]

---

21. *Government of India Resolution on Industrial Policy*, April 6, 1948, Para-4.

22. *Ibid.*, Para-4.

23. *Ibid.*, Para-5.

The Industrial Policy, 1948, can be recorded as a sincere effort of the government towards the direct interference in the field of industry and a radical departure from the *Lessez Faire* economic policy followed by the British Rulers in India.

The Articles-39 (b) and (c) of the Constitution of India adopted on 26th January, 1950, also favoured to the state planning and interference. The constitution directed the state under these articles to secure "that the ownership and control of the material resources of the community are so distributed as best to subserve the common goods," and that the operation of the economic system does not result in the concentration of wealth and means of production to the common detriment.[24]

As per the directive of the Indian constitution, the Government of India set up the Planning Commission in 1950 by passing a resolution regarding it. In December, 1952, the Planning Commission indicated the need for a rapid expansion of economic and social responsibilities of the state which "need not involve complete nationalisation of means of production or elimination of private agencies in agriculture or business and industry, only a progressive winding of the public sector and re-orientation of the private sector to the need of planned economy."[25] The plan stated that "the private and the public sectors cannot be looked upon anything like two separate entities. They are and must function as parts of a single organism."[26] This approach enunciated in the plan was to fill the gap between public and private sectors by the latter becoming more socially-oriented.

The Congress Party passed an important resolution captioned 'Socialist Pattern of Society' in its session in 1954. Highlighting the need and importance of public sector in India, Pandit Nehru remarked on the resolution, "we cannot progress except by State initiative and except by enlarging the public sector and except also by controlling the private sector in a measure."[27] As it was

24. Quoted by Laxmi Narayan in Principal & *Practice of Public Enterprise Management*, 1992, S. Chand & Co. Ltd., New Delhi, p. 21.

25. *First Five Year Plan*, p. 31-32.

26. *Ibid.*, p. 33.

27. Quoted by P. Prasad, *op. cit.*, p. 119.

a clear indication to select the measures for the economic development of the country in future, it could be treated as a turning point in the history of Indian economy related to public sector.

In the meantime, an important resolution was passed by the Lok Sabha on 21st December 1954. After detailed deliberations in the Parliament on economic policy, the highest representative body of the people of the country decided that the prime objective of India's economic policy should be to establish a 'Socialist Pattern of Society'. The resolution referred to the directive principles of the State Policy. "The adoption of the socialist pattern of society as the national objective, as well as the need for planned and rapid development, required that all industries of basic and strategic importance, or in the nature of public utility services should be in the public sector. Other industries which are essential and require investment on a large scale which only the state in the present circumstances, could provide, have also to be in the public sector. The State has, therefore, to assume direct responsibility for the future development of industries over a wide area."[28] It also lays down that the state will progressively assume a predominant and direct responsibility for setting up new industrial undertakings and for the development of transport and Infrastructure facilities, and it will also undertake state trading on an increasing rate. Side by side, the resolution also stressed the role of the private sector as an important agency in the planned development of the country.

In order to fulfil the objectives of the socialistic pattern of society and to accelerate the rate of economic growth as well as to speed up industrialisation, to develop heavy machine making industries, it was deemed essential to expand the public sector. It was also necessary for increasing employment improving standard of living of the masses, reducing disparities in income and wealth and for preventing private monopoly and concentration of economic power.

Industrial Policy 1956

By accepting the above mentioned challenges the Government

---

28. Extracts from *Policy Resolution*, quoted by Gupta, R.K., Public Enterprises in India, 1978, p. 32.

of India announced its new Industrial Policy on 30th April 1956. Under this policy, the industries were divided into three basic categories :

In the first category, 17 basic strategic industries were kept. The development of these industries was the exclusive responsibility of the State. "These 'industries are given in Schedule — 'A' of the resolution and consist of the following :"[29]

(1) Arms and Ammunition and allied items of defence equipments;

(2) Atomic Energy;

(3) Iron and Steel;

(4) Heavy castings and forgings of Iron and Steel;

(5) Heavy plant and machinery required for iron and steel production for mining, for machine tools, manufacture and for such basic industries as may be specified by the Central Government;

(6) Heavy Electrical Plant including large hydraulic and steam turbines;

(7) Coal and Lignite;

(8) Mineral Oils;

(9) Mining of iron ore, manganese ore, chrome ore, Gypsum, Sulphur, Gold and Diamond;

(10) Mining and Processing of copper Lead, Zinc, Tin Molybdenum and Walframe;

(11) Minerals specified in the schedule to the Atomic Energy (Control of Production and Use order, 1955);

(12) Aircraft;

(13) Air Transport;

(14) Railway Transport;

(15) Ship Building;

(16) Telephone and Telephone Cable, Telegraph and Wireless Apparatus.(excluding Radio Receiving sets);

(17) Generation and distribution of electricity.

---

29. *Second Five Year Plan*, 1955, p. 50.

In the second category, 12 industries were included in which provision was made to be operated by public and private enterprises both side by side. But it will be progressively state-owned in which the state will generally take the initiative in establishing new undertakings. The private sector is also given the opportunity to develop in this field, either at its own or with state participation. "The industries relating to this category have been included in Schedule — 'B' of the resolution and consist of the following :"[30]

(1) All other minerals except 'Minor Minerals' as defined in Section 3 of the Mineral Concession Rules, 1949;

(2) Aluminium and other non-ferrous metals not 'included 'in Schedule — 'A';

(3) Machine Tools;

(4) Ferro-alloys and tool steel;

(5) Basic and intermediate products required by chemical industries, such as manufacture of drugs, dyestuffs and plastics;

(6) Antibiotics and other essential drugs;

(7) Fertilisers;

(8) Synthetic rubber;

(9) Carbonisation of coal;

(10) Chemical pulp;

(11) Road transport;

(12) Sea Transport.

The remaining all other industries, that were not included in Schedule — 'A' and 'B', were kept in the category third. Though the development of these industries was left to the initiative of private sector, the door was kept open for the state to start any industry of this category.

The resolutions adopted in Industrial Policy, 1956 have been accepted as the basic guideline for the industrial development of the country under Five Year Plans. Thus, the development of

30. *Second Five Year Plan*, 1955, p. 50.

public sector was given a matter of prime importance to develop the Indian economy after independence and it assumed huge responsibilities for the development of industrial undertakings in India.

The Industrial Licensing Policy Enquiry Committee was constituted in 1967 under the Chairmanship of Mr. S. Dutta. The Committee was assigned to review the usefulness of the licensing system in the light of objectives of Industrial Policy Resolution, 1956. At the same time, the Administrative Reforms Commission was also set up to observe the requirement of administrative reformation.

Industrial Licensing Policy 1970

In view of the recommendations of the Administrative Reforms Commission and Industrial Licensing Policy Enquiry Committee, the government announced its new Licensing Policy in February, 1970. The policy divided the industries into six categories. The industries involving heavy investment of more than Rs. 5 crore were included in core sector. Under this sector, 17 basic and strategic industries, that were specified in Schedule — 'A' of the Industrial Policy Resolution of 1956, were reserved for the public sector while other nine more industries included in this sector were kept under the option of joint sector to establish any new unit of these nine industries.

Industrial Licensing Policy 1973

The scope of public sector was further expanded by the declaration of new licensing policy of the Government of India in February, 1973. It was the modified form of Licensing Policy, 1970. The policy further expanded the core sector. The policy lays down, "In the context to the Fifth Five Year Plan, the State will have to take direct responsibility for the further development of industries over a wide field in order to promote the cardinal objective to grow social justice, self-reliance and satisfaction of the basic minimum need."[31]

The importance of the new Licensing Policy in regard to the

31. *Hindustan Times,* Extract Policy Resolution, 1973, February 3.

expansion of public sector was expressed by the then Prime Minister Mrs. Indira Gandhi stating that — "the recent announcement of the Industrial Licensing Policy assigned as expanded role of the public sector in new areas and direction. The private sector has neither the capacity nor the will to take up the production of those items which present an immediate problem for the people, those items which form the base and which take a long time in producing result."[32] However, the industries defined under core sector were exclusively reserved for the public sector in the Licensing Policy, 1970 and were allowed the entrance of the private sector under the policy of 1973. This was a major change over the 1970's policy.

Industrial Policy 1977

After independence, the first non-congress government came to power at centre in 1977. The Government of Janata Party under the Prime Ministership of Sri Morarji Desai announced its Industrial Policy on 23rd December, 1977. "The policy envisaged Public Enterprises as a means of socialising the means of production in strategic areas for providing a countervailing force to the growth of large houses and large scale enterprises in the private sector."[33] The new policy also contemplated a greater role for public enterprises specially in the field of production of important and strategic goods of basic nature. Apart from this, the policy directed this sector to act as a stabilising force for maintaining essential supplies for the consumer and encouraging a wide range of ancillary industries in the small-scale and cottage industries sector. The policy emphasised to operate the public enterprises on profitable and efficient lines so that an adequate return on the investment made in this sector can be achieved.

Industrial Policy 1980

The policy announced by the Janata Government could not be operated for a longer period, because of the sudden fall of the Government. The new government headed by Mrs. Indira Gandhi came to power at Centre and announced the new Industrial

32. *Lok Udyog*, May 1969, Prime Minister on Public Sector.

33. Narain, Laxmi, *op. cit.*, p. 25.

Policy on 23rd of July, 1980. In its resolution, the public sector was recalled as a people sector. The Policy stated that Public sector is an important part of our economy and there was a great contribution of this sector in formulation of additional resources, increase in opportunity of employment and in rapid economic growth. Therefore, it is most essential to improve the working of the public sector for which a time bound programme should be adopted. It was also decided to give the priority of improving the efficiency of the units running on continuous losses. For this, the establishment of separate managerial cadre in various facets of the management like production, marketing, finance, personnel and management information system was strongly advocated. Thus, it was the first important sign of ideological change of the government in the policies adopted earlier concerning the public sector. Now the emphasis shifted from haphazard and unwisely expansion of public sector undertakings to their efficient management. This was a turning point for the public sector in the present context.

In the meantime the Arjun Sen Gupta Committee was constituted by the government to review the policy for public enterprises. The committee submitted its report in 1985. The report comprises many important recommendations of fundamental change. The committee strongly advocated to ensure real autonomy for the public enterprises. "It is recognised by all that on paper, management of public enterprises enjoy larger autonomy, sometimes much more than even by the private sector management. However, in practice, informal and formal involvement of ministries and departments take place in areas wholly within the decision making powers of public enterprises."[34] On involvement of the Government in public enterprises operations, the committee recommended that "it is necessary to evolve a set of rules and conventions by which the Government can help in the better functioning of Public Enterprises by reducing the points of intervention without minimising the Government's right to have needed information for evaluating performance. The government should primarily be concerned with overall strategic planning and

34. *Arjun Sen Gupta Report*, 1985. (Quoted by Dharneja Nand, *Productivity*, Vol. 35, No. 1) April-June, 1994, p. 144.

policy, rather than with day-to-day functioning of the enterprise."[35] The committee also recommended the implementation of system of Memorandum of Understanding (MOU); to improve the performance of public enterprises by increasing the operational autonomy. In regard to financial autonomy, the committee recommended that enterprises not reserved for public sector should have financial autonomy in terms of raising resources from banks, or capital market. "Their plans be integrated into the National Plan only in indicative sense and such units would continue to be governed by the indicative and regulatory framework of planning as application for all similar private sector units."[36]

Industrial Policy 1990

The second non-congress Government of Janata Dal came to power and announced its new Industrial Policy on May 31, 1990. In this policy statement, an effort was made to permit blanket liberalisation with a view to accelerating the growth of medium and large-scale sector, though the preference was given to promote small-scale and agro-based industries. So far as public sector is concerned, the policy does not include any new idea of vital importance. Due to the sudden fall of the Janta Dal Government, the decisions could not be carried out more effectively.

Till ninetees, except a very few exceptions like Industrial Policy, 1977 and 1990, the Indian economy was governed mainly on the broad guidelines of Industrial Policy 1956 which was the essence of pro-public sector. In the meantime, the scenario of world economy was changing very rapidly. Iran-Iraq-War, unsuccessful mission of U.S.S.R. interference in Afganistan, end of the Cold War, weakening of Nonallign Movement were some of the important events that weakened the socialistic thought the world over. However, the greatest blow to this thought came from the victory of trade union rights in Poland, acceptance of market economy to a large extent by China after the death of Mao-Tse-Tunga, re-unification of both East and West Germany and lastly the collapse of Communism in Soviet Russia.

35. *Arjun Sen Gupta Report*, 1984 (Quoted by Dhanneja Nand, *Productivity*, Vol. 35 No. 1), April-June, 1994, p. 145.

36. *Ibid*.

The concept of economic liberalisation arose as a new dawn on the socio-political horizon of the world. Many countries, mainly underdeveloped, were compelled to restructure their economic policies in the light of the current changes occurring in the world. They were bound to minimise the protection given to inefficient and loss making public sector units. Now the public sector units were expected to compete in the world market on their own. Thus, the profit concept became the matter of prime importance for the public sector, like private sector.

All these events also affected the economic and industrial conditions and policies adopted in India. Now the government was not in favour to run the state enterprises at all costs, even if they went on incurring recurring losses. The market liberalisation became the compulsive need of Indian economy. It is the 'era' of a fundamental turning in Indian industrial scene. Considering all these facts, the government took some major decisions to restructure the public sector by announcing its new Industrial Policy on 24th July, 1991.

Industrial Policy 1991

After the departure of the short regime of the second non-Congress Government of Janta Dal at the Centre, the Congress Government came to power again in 1991. The government announced its new industrial policy on 24th July, 1991. The main object of the policy was to take forward the Indian economy with the changing conditions of the world economic affairs — by liberalising the market. In new industrial policy, the Government decided to limit its role in the field of business and industry by stating that........ "Government will endeavour to abolish the monopoly of any sector or any individual enterprise in any field of manufacture, except on strategic consideration and open all manufacturing activities to competition."[37]

To fulfil the above mentioned objectives, the Government has abolished the industrial licensing system for all other industries having no bar of capital investment except eighteen industries of strategic and defence importance. Later on from 14th April 1993,

37. *Industrial Policy Statement*, 24th July, 1991.

it was reduced to fifteen only. The number of industries considered under core sector and reserved only for public sector was also reduced to eight only. Besides, the ratio of foreign capital investment in FERA companies was increased from 40 per cent to 51 per cent. The other important measures of liberalisation include ammendment of MRTP Act, permission for foreign technology agreements in high priority industries, liberal provisions for hiring foreign technicians. With the declaration of the industrial policy statement, the government adopted a new approach to public enterprises. The decision was taken to run this sector on a business line with a greater autonomy in future. "The government will ensure that the public sector plays its rightful role in evolving the socio-economic scenario of the country. Government will ensure that the public sector is run on business lines. Further.... Public sector which are chronically sick and which are unlikely to be turned around will for the formulation of revival or rehabilitation schemes be referred to the Board for Industrial and Financial Reconstruction (BIFR) or other similar high level institutions created for the purpose. The policy also decided to improve the performance of public sector by granting greater autonomy. There will be a greater thrust on performance improvement through the Memorandum of Understanding (MOU).system, through which management would be granted greater autonomy and will be held accountable."[38]

The policy also comprises the priorities of the development of public sector in future. The industries relating to basic goods and services, development of mineral and oil resources, the areas which are essential for the long run development of the country and the manufacture of strategic importance were kept in the priority list for the development of this sector in future. For the first time in the history of public sector since independence, the provision was made to sell the share capital of the public enterprises directly in the market upto a certain limit. In order to raise resources and encourage a wider public participation, a part of the government share-holding in the public sector would be offered to mutual funds, financial institutions, general public and workers.

38. Industrial Policy Statement, 24th July 1991.

Thus, it is clear that the announcement of Industrial Policy, 1991, brought about a fundamental change in the scenario of public sector undertakings in India. The main objective of all previous industrial policies declared from time to time was to accelerate the industrial growth of the country. But by the end of the Seventh Five-Year-Plan as stated earlier, a world-wide competition came into picture with the economic liberalisation. Being an important segment of economy, the public sector also has to face this challenge. This would have been possible only by adopting modernisation process and new technologies. The generation of adequate internal surpluses was considered to be a must. Therefore, the main thrust in the policy statement, 1991, was given on profit earning by improving over-all performance of the public sector and granting greater autonomy.

Public Sector at a Glance

In continuation of the policies framed from time to time for the development of public sector, it is essential to give a composite look on the physical growth of this sector during Five Year Plans. The first government of independent India decided to accelerate the economic growth by adopting planning as a measure. Simultaneously, the role of public sector was also determined to achieve goal and to devolve a socialist pattern of society. This sector was assigned the crucial task to achieve the objective of the planning by removing the regional imbalances and equating the wealth distribution. "The Planning Commission demanded a rapid expansion of the economic and social responsibilities of the state to satisfy the legitimate expectations of people."[39] The table given below shows a comprehensive picture of the growth of public sector enterprises in terms of numbers and investment therein, under the Five Year Plans.

39. Gupta, R.K., *Public Enterprises in India*, 1978, p. 46.

TABLE 1

Growth Table of Public Enterprises

Plans	*As on*	*No. of Enterprises*	*Total Investment (Rs. In crores)*
First Five Year Plan	1 April 1951	5	29
Second Five Year Plan	1 April 1956	21	81
Third Five Year Plan	1 April 1961	47	948
Fourth Five Year Plan	1 April 1969	84	3,897
Fifth Five Year Plan	1 April 1974	122	6,237
Sixth Five Year Plan	1 April 1980	179	18,150
Seventh Five Year Plan	1 April 1985	215	42,673
Eighth Five Year Plan			
As On	31 March 1991	246	1,13,896
As On	31 March 1992	246	1,35,871
As On	31 March 1994	246	1,46,971

Note : Dates are the commencement dates of the Plans.

Source : *Government of India, Public Enterprises Survey*, 1993-94, Vol. 1.

Analysis

The above mentioned table shows that the investment in Central Public Enterprises has grown appreciably over the years. There were only five public enterprises with an investment of Rs. 29 crore only on April 1951. The number of enterprises increased to 246 as on 31, March 1994 with an investment of Rs. 1,46,971 crore. The table comprises the total investment made in terms of share capital and long-term loans of the various groups of the public enterprises excluding Banking and Financial

Institutions. It Is clear from the table that there was a consistent increase in the number of new units by 16 in First Plan, 26 in Second Plan, 37 in Third Plan and 38 in Fourth Plan. The maximum number of new units were established during Fifth Plan *i.e.,* 57. It was the period in which the public enterprises got maximum encouragement in terms of number as well as the ratio of outlays. There was a stagnation in their growth during Eighth Plan period. There was more or less an equivalent rate of growth to third Plan's growth rate during this. It was the result of strict measures adopted by the Government regarding further expansion of this sector blindly as incorporated in its New Industrial Policy, 1991.

So far as the investment in public enterprises is concerned, there was a galloping increase during the second plan when it recorded an increase of about twelve times over to the investment of the previous plan. This was mainly because of the initiation of many new and big projects under the public sector in the light of the industrial policy resolution, 1956. The table also shows a constant and significant increase from the third paln to the seventh plan which is conpatible to its physical growth recorded during this. But it is important to mention that "only top 10 giant enterprises covered the 53.6 per cent share *i.e.* Rs. 71,107 crore out of the total investment of Rs. 1,46,971 crore in 246 total enterprises as on 31, March, 1994."[40]

Financial Performance of Public Enterprises

The following table shows the financial performance of Central Public Enterprises with respect to capital employed and rate of return achieved over to capital in terms of both gross profit and net profit, the period, for which the study is made, covers from Fifth Five Year Plan to Seventh Five Year Plan *i.e.,* 1974-75 to 1992-93 :

40. *Government of India, Public Enterprises Survey*, 1993-94, Vol. I. p. 9.

TABLE 2

Financial Performance of Central Public Enterprises (Running)

(Rs. in crores)

Year	*No. of Units*	*Capital Employed*	*Gross Profit Before Tax*	*Net Profit Before Tax*	*Net Profit After Tax*	*Rate of Return*	
						Gross Profit to Capital Employed (%)	*Net Profit after Tax to Capital Employed (%)*
1	2	3	4	5	6	7	8
1974-75	120	6,627	559	312	184	8.4	2.8
1975-76	121	8,884	668	306	129	7.6	1.5
1976-77	149	10,887	1028	421	184	9.4	1.7
1977-78	155	12,130	915	160	(-92)	7.5	(-0.8)
1978-79	159	13,969	1071	185	(-40)	7.7	(-0.3)
1979-80	169	16,182	1229	255	(-47)	7.6	(-0.3)
1980-81	168	18,207	1418	19	(-203)	7.8	(-1.1)
1981-82	188	21,935	2654	1025	446	12.1	2.0
1982-83	193	26,590	3469	1547	618	13.1	2.3

(*Contd...*)

TABLE 2 (*Contd.*)

1	2	3	4	5	6	7	8
1983-84	201	29,856	3565	1480	240	11.9	0.8
1984-85	207	36,382	4,628	2,099	909	12.7	2.5
1985-86	211	42,965	5,287	2,173	1,172	12.3	2.8
1986-87	214	51,835	6,521	3,101	1,771	12.6	3.4
1987-88	220	55,617	6,940	3,353	2,030	12.5	3.6
1988-89	226	67,629	8,572	4,404	2,993	12.7	4.4
1989-90	233	84,760	10,622	5,293	3,789	12.5	4.5
1990-91	236	1,01,702	11,359	3,820	2,368	11.2	2.3
1991-92	237	1,17,991	13,675	4,003	2,355	11.6	2.0
1992-93	237	1,39,933	15,978	5,200	3,396	11.4	2.4

Source : *Public Enterprise Survey*, 1993-94, Vol. I and earlier issues.

The above-mentioned table shows the trend of financial performance of the running Central Public Enterprises since 1974-75. There were only 120 running units in 1974-75 which grew up to 237 in 1992-93. In the Fifth Plan Period (1974-75 to 1977-78), the percentage of gross profit to capital employed varied between 7.5 per cent to 9.4 per cent. During 1980-81 this ration showed a distinct picture of improvement. It rose from 7.8 per cent in 1980-81 to 13.1 per cent in 1982-83. Thereafter, the ration of gross profit as a ratio of capital employed, ranged in between 11.2 per cent in 1990-91 to 12.7 per cent in 1988-89. In 1992-93 this was only 11.4 per cent.

So far the ratio of net profit after tax to capital employed is concerned, it has declined consistently since 1974-75 to 1980-81 not only this but there was a recurring net loss of percentage in between 197-78 to 1980-81 which shows a very poor performance of these enterprises. Thereafter it improved considerably as 2.0 per cent in 1981-82 to 4.5 per cent in 1989-90 except in 1983-84 when it stood at only 0.8 per cent. Reviewing the situation, *Public Enterprises Survey* (1989-90) reveals : "In absolute terms net profits after tax of Central Government Public Enterprises rose substantially from Rs. 2,993 crore in 1988-89 to Rs. 3,781 crore in 1989-90. The rate of return, as measured by net profits to capital employed rose to 4.5 per cent in 1989-90 which is the highest in the decade. However, as in previous years, the petroleum sector enterprises contributed the overwhelming bulk of these profits Rs. 2,899 crore out of the total Rs. 3,782 crore in 1989-90 (76.6 per cent of total). Thus, the 200 odd non-petroleum enterprises contributed a meagre sum of Rs. 833 crore. While this reflected an improvement over the net profit of Rs. 431 crore in 1988-89, the ratio of net profits to capital employed in non-petroleum sector enterprises was barely 1.3 per cent in 1989-90."[41]

However, the net rate of return declined from 4.5 per cent in 1989-96 to 2.2 per cent in 1990-91 the lowest since 1984-85 and it declined further to 2.0 per cent in 1991-92 but with a slight improvement in 1992-93 it stood at 2.4 per cent. There was an acute foreign exchange crisis and resource crunch and over all

41. *Public Enterprises Survey*, 1989-90, Vol. I.

economic detoriation in 1991-92 which also affected public sector adversely with respect to its financial performance.

From the above mentioned fact one thing is noticeable that there is a very poor return from a large number of non-petroleum units of public enterprises as most of the units are running on recurring losses. The continuous poor performance shown by public sector enterprises has brought this sector at a serious point today. Ideological discussions and debates are going on whether this sector should be improved by hook or by crook and be continued or should be handed over to private hands. The government has also shown a keen interest to improve this sector by adopting many new measures in recent years. On the other hand, the government has also made it clear that she will not hesitate to choose the second option for such units which are chronically sick and are not showing any sign of improvement. Whatever the result may be, one thing is very clear that now this sector has no option but to improve its efficiency.

The continuous poor performance of the public sector with respect to resource generation and the adoption of the liberalisation policy of the Government of India has also put the Indian public sector undertakings on the cross roads. Hence, the need for ample reformative measures with regard to these public sector undertakings.

Reformative Measures taken by the Government

In pursuance of the Industrial Policy, 1991, a techno-economic approach was adopted to review the performance of public enterprises. The enterprises were divided into different categories on the basis of their performance levels, characteristics of market structure, efficiency and their social obligations. An evaluation matrix was also developed by the government which could make the evaluation more objective and easier to comprehend and also to bring out the policy options for each category of public sector undertakings simultaneously. The following important steps were taken by the government :

(a) **Revival and Rehabilitation Programme.** On the basis of review made on the above lines, the sick enterprises were identified and a monograph on the performance status of Central Public Enterprises was prepared. It was submitted before the Parliament for a discussion in December 1991. The government decided to refer the chronically sick enterprises to the Board of Industrial and Financial Reconstruction (BIFR) under the Sick Industrial Companies Act (SICA), 1985, for the formulation of revival and rehabilitation scheme. The Act SICA has since been amended to make mandatory the referral of sick public sector enterprises to BIFR on the same line as the private sector enterprises. On the basis of result of 1991-92, 50 Central Public Sector Enterprises have been identified as sick out of which 38 have already been registered by BIFR.

(b) **Disinvestment Policy.** In order to raise resources and encourage wider participation of public and to promote greater accountability, the decision was taken to offer up to 20 per cent of the government equity in selected enterprises for the sale to Mutual Funds, financial Investment Institutions, workers and general public. In pursuance of this decision, the government selected 31 public sector enterprises having a good track record of performance and offered a part of their equity varying from 5 per cent to 20 per cent for sale to public sector Mutual Funds and Financial Institutions. The equity was offered in bundles as there was no established market price for these shares. The total number of shares disinvested in two bunches during 1991-92 constituted only 8 per cent of the government holding in 30 public enterprises. The amount raised was 3038 crore against the budget announcement of Rs. 2,500 crore for the year. Further in March, 1994, the government invited tenders for the sale of shares of seven Central Public Enterprises. For the first time, the foreign institutional investors were allowed to bid for the share. The minimum offer amount was reduced to Rs. 25,000 from the earlier level of Rs. 1,00,000 (one lakh). The public sector undertakings floated capital issues for an amount aggregating to Rs. 5311 crore through issues of equity and bonds in 1993-94. It was a rise of Rs. 3,119 crore (142.3 per cent) over that of the previous year.

(c) **Financial Appraisal.** The financial appraisal was taken as an important yardstick to measure the performance of these enterprises because the decision had already been taken to run these on a commercial line. The analysis of performance of these enterprises with reference to such ratios as gross profit to capital employed, sales to capital employed, etc. has been taken into consideration. This is done with the consideration of the fact that the public sector has to discharge a number of other socio-economic obligations. The performance appraisal covers also the internal resource generation for financing the plan, contribution to public exchequer, management development, development of backward regions, employment and employees welfare measures, foreign exchange earnings, import substitution effort and other related matters that present a comprehensive picture of this sector.

(d) **Adoption of Memorandum of Understanding (MOU).** The government took a policy decision to adopt the concept of Memorandum of Understanding (MOU) for the improvement of performance of public sector undertakings. It is an instrument which defines the relationship between government and public sector undertakings clearly. The MOU also clarifies the respective role of public sector undertakings as well as the government in order to achieve better performance. It was an effective interface between both the government and management of public sector enterprises for ensuring operational autonomy with corresponding accountability. The emphasis is on achieving the negotiated and agreed objective rather than interfering in day-to-day affairs.

The Industrial Policy, 1991 extended the scope of the policy of MOU to all public sector enterprises, except for those that were referred to the BIFR. The main objective of MOU policy is to reduce the quantity of control and increase the quality of accountability. This is sought to be done by specifying explicity in clear terms the measurable goals and giving the enterprises greater operational autonomy to improve them. Thus, for the first time, in the history of public sector enterprises, an attempt was made to manage these enterprises by objective rather than control them by holding them accountable for procedure.

In 1991-92, 71 public enterprises signed MOU with their Administrative Ministries. Out of 58 enterprises evaluated, 25 were rated as "Excellent" and 21 as 'Very Good.' In the year 1992-93, 98 enterprises signed this 97 enterprises were evaluated out of which 37 were rated as "Excellent" and 35 as 'Very Good'. This implies that the level of performance of nearly 75 per cent of public sector enterprises working under the MOUs has improved and shows the positive effect of the policy.

Now the MOU policy has become market-oriented. A provision has been made that the Performance Budget of MOU targets should synchronise and the MOU targets must reflect an improvement over the previous years planned budget target in order to be categorised as 'Very Good.' Besides, the Weight for profit and profit related criteria in the MOUs for 1992-93 were fixed as around 50 per cent in order to bring about a congruence between MOU scores and financial performance.

Conclusion

At initial stage, the public sector undertakings were assigned a crucial task to lay down the foundation for a vast and varied industrial growth in independent India. The adoption of planning and socialist pattern of society approach also raised the compulsive need of this sector. The public sector had carried out its responsibilities during the First, Second and Third Five Year Plans by developing indian industries substantively. Many projects of basic importance like iron and steel, oil and minerals and light and heavy engineering were set up during this period which gave a solid base to Indian economy undoubtedly. To some extent we can say that up to seventies this sector was run on a monopolistic line because of the unquestionable support and protection of the government. Bureaucratic management, undesired interference of the politicians, over employment, ineffective control and lack of professional approach led this sector to continuous low productive lines and pushed it to recurring losses of huge amount. Most of the public enterprises failed to achieve the important objective of resource generation.

However, some important events on the political and economic scenario of the world (as discussed in the previous part) have changed the framework of economic policies of the various countries specially developing ones. Concept of market liberalisation, globalisation and privatisation arose as a new dawn on the world's economic horizon and brought about a new challenge before the economic planners. In the light of all these affairs, it has become a compulsive need for the Government of India to review its economic policy, so that economy could be carried forward successfully by facing all these challenges. The adoption of many corrective measures under the new Industrial Policy, 1991 and decision to run the public sector on commercial lines as private sector shows the fundamental changes in the outlook of the government in consonance with the crying need of the day.

In the meantime, the dismal performance of public sector enterprises with respect to resource generation evoked strong criticism from various quarters. Now even the planners are advocating privatisation as the measure to combat the problem, with the conviction that the malaise paralysing loss making units would be dispelled under the above nursing of private sector. Thus, we can say that today public sector is at cross roads. Therefore, it is the responsibility of all those who work in this sector to adopt a total quality approach to prove them best and nothing less than that. At the same time, continuous efforts must go into restructuring the public sector enterprises to make them more productive and viable rather than blindly going in for privatisation.

2

Budgeting — Concept and Importance

Budget and Budgeting

Before entering into the detailed conceptual analysis of the budgeting also termed as profit planning and control, and its important fundamentals, it is imperative to mention the meaning of budget. Budget is a financial and narrative expression of the expected results from the planned decisions. Since such expressions explicitly state the goals in terms of time expectations and expected financial results for each major segment of an entity, it is called budget. Mr. Scott, J.A. defined budget as "A financial and quantitative statement prepared prior to a defined period of time, of the policy to be persued during that period for the purpose of achieving a given objective."[1]

Budget is not merely an instrument for providing ceiling on expenditure to be incurred in a particular year, but it has an important role to play in discharging of the essential functions of management in a most efficient manner. In this context, Dr. I.M. Pandey has mentioned...... "one systematic approach to facilitate the effective management performance is profit planning and control or budgeting."[2] Further at the sixth International Congress for Scientific Management, Ronal Dunkerely states....... "budget coordinates sales, manufacturing and finance and enables management to decide policy with some knowledge of the results thereof, and provides an objective and measure of success, provides a stimulus and emphasises collective effort and the

1. Scott, J.A., *Budgetary Control and Standard Cost*, 1970, p. 12.
2. Pandey, I.M., *Financial Management,* Vikash Publishing House Pvt. Ltd. New Delhi, 1979, p. 454.

profit objectives.... executives to think and think as a group." Thus, the budgets are designed to carry out the various managerial functions, *i.e.*, planning, evaluating performance, coordinating activities, execution of plans, communicating, motivating and authorising.

Budgeting

The term budgeting is applied to the system of management control and accounting in which all operations are forecast and planned ahead and the actual results are compared with the planned one. So we can say that the word budgeting is wider than a 'budget one' because it includes the analysis of deviations of actual results also. Budgeting often used in the context as comprehensive profit planning and control may be broadly defined as a systematic and formalised approach for accomplishing the important functions of management, *i.e.*, planning, co-ordination and control. In earlier years, the common view of budgeting was the notion that accountants in a firm should be assigned the responsibility for developing a "financial evaluation of what the future year probably will hold."[3] In recent years, there has been a tendency to view budgeting as a 'mathematical model' for the entity. But the most relevant aspect of the concept of budgeting is that it is an integral aspect of the management process. Basically it is the decision-making tool of the management with a critical behavioural implication which offers a systematic practical and proven approach of the management process.

More specifically it involves the development and application of :

(i) Broad and long range objectives for enterprises;

(ii) Specification of enterprise goals;

(iii) A long-range profit plan developed in broad terms;

(iv) A short range profit plan detailed by relevant responsibilities;

(v) A system of periodic performance report and detailed by assigned responsibilities and

(vi) Follow-up procedures.

---

3. Welsch, Glenn. A., *Budgeting Profit Planning and Control*, 1976.

Thus, "budgeting control involves the evaluation of plans in financial terms and the comparison of actual results with the plans made."[4]

Budgeting is a continuous process of discharging important managerial responsibilities as to get the desired goals of an enterprise. It is one of the important practices of management to utilise the individual and group efforts in a co-ordinated and rational way. Further, it is a continuous process and it can never be considered as the final and ultimate. It is always subject to revision in context to the prevailing conditions.

The term 'Budgeting' encompasses the planning and control theory of management. As Welsch states...... "the primary success factor in an enterprise is the competence of management to plan and to control enterprise activities. This notion says that management earns its bread and butter only if it can, in fact, plan and control in ways that determine the long range destiny of the enterprise."[5]

In the light of this statement, the entire managerial activities relating to budgeting in an enterprise may be classified as follows :

1. Planning
2. Control
3. Co-ordination

Planning

The planning is a decision-making process of management that provides guidelines for making day-to-day operational decisions. The management planning has been defined as the design of a desired future state for an entity and of effective ways of bringing it about.[6]

The establishment of the objectives of an enterprise represents the most fundamental level of decision-making in the planning

4. J Batty, *Corporate Planning and Budgetary Control*, (Macdonal and Evans Ltd., London), 1970, p. 43.
5. Weslsch, Clenn, A., *Budgeting : Profit Planning and Control*, 1976, p. 9.
6. Russell L. Ackoff, *A Concept of Corporate Planning*, New York, 1970, p. 1.

process. In order to establish the foundation for attainment of the enterprise objectives and the specific goals, the management must develop long-range and short-range strategies to be persued by the enterprise. The detailed level of planning takes place when the budget is prepared.

Control

The second important step of budgeting is to know the operational progress of the planned objectives. It is known as control function of management. It can simply be defined as the action needed to assure objectives, plans, policies and standards to be attained. Control pre-supposes feed forward that is, objectives, plans, policies and standards have been developed and communicated to the performance responsibility centres. The effective control must be exercised at the point of action or at the time of commitment. The comparison of actual results with planned goals and set standards shows the effectiveness of control during a specific period.

The budgeting-practices have gained wide acceptance in regards to overall control in an enterprise. The important ways, in which the budgetary process aids control, are the measurement of actual results with planned goals and standards and the reporting of that measurement. It extends to all areas of operations and the responsibility centres in the enterprise. Further Mr. Russel pointed out that the control process involves four important Steps :[7]

(i) Predicting the outcomes of decisions in the form of performance measures;

(ii) Collecting information on actual performance;

(iii) Comparison of actual results with predicted performance and

(iv) When a decision is shown to have been deficient, correcting the procedure that produced it and correcting its consequences where possible.

---

7. Russel, L. Ackoff, *A Concept of Corporate Planning*, New York, John Wiley & Sons, 1970, p. 1.

The control aspect of budgeting makes it possible for management to feel the pulse of the enterprise all the times. Through this, management can be able to know the real position of progress with respect to the overall objectives as well as specific goal. If any deviation is located, the corrective measures can be taken.

Co-ordination

People exchange their views, ideas, prejudices and attitudes when they work together. Co-ordination involves the interpersonal relationship of the people in the work situation. When it is understood by the managers as to how their particular action contributes to the overall objectives of the enterprise, the basic foundation for co-ordination is established. The continuous interchange of plans, policies and ideas is essential. The budgeting emphasises goal congruence through realistic planning, dynamic control and effective communication, by which it establishes the basis for the harmony, synchronisation and unity of effort on continuing basis through effective co-ordination. In the budgeting-process, all aspects of a business are converted into a common language so that each and every manager may feel the significance of the part he can play in achieving the objectives. In the proper form of budgeting programmes, the fully co-ordinated and systematic approach to the financial planning is adopted at the concerned responsibility centres.

In this way, the budgeting is a comprehensive system to co-ordinate all aspects of the management process, carefully knitting together the loose ends of management and operations. It makes the task of management more systematic, more effective and more rewarding and can be applied so as to impart high degree of flexibility in managing the affairs of an enterprise.

INGREDIENTS OF BUDGETING

The ingredients, that are crucial for clear understanding and effective application of the budgeting, may be enumerated as follows :

1. Budget Manual

It constitutes the design of budget schedule, methods of

completing such schedules and routine computations. Budget manual is an embodyment of the rules and regulations regarding budget preparation and budget administration. It is the most important document comprising the objectives, provisions, methodology and functionaries of budgeting to be adopted in an organisation. It becomes a testament for all budgetary activities in the organisation. It provides all sorts of rules and regulations with regards to the development of budget and its administration. Strict adherence to the provisions of budget manual is essential to the effective implementation of budgeting activities unless and until circumstances necessitate otherwise.

2. Techniques of Budgeting

These are special approaches and methods of developing information for managerial use in the process of decision-making. Normally techniques, that are used, are the methods of forecasting sales volume, approaches in resolving the sales-production inventory problems, break-even analysis, cash flow analysis and variables of budget Procedures.

3. Budget Committee

It is the prime body of the organisation to discharge all budgetary functions. The Committee is headed by the Chief Executive of the organisation who performs this job with the co-ordination of all departmental heads. The staff work of the committee is carried out by the incharge of the committee, generally designated as Budget Officer. But it is a common principle that all the executives of the enterprise have a responsibility for the budget of the activities which they control. Apart from interpreting the guiding decisions of the Budget Committee, the Budget Officer is also expected to do the job of advising the responsible executives with a view to securing budget which is compatible with that of the other sections.

Development of Budget or Budget Preparation. The following are the important steps of budget preparation :

(a) *Determination of Budget Level* : Before proceeding to the preparation of budgets, the level of attainment, which forms the basis of budget, must be defined. The main consideration should be given to forecast objectively the factors over which the business has no control, *i.e.*, purchase prices, national wage rate and other external factors for the period under review. The special attention is required to fix the standard levels. These standards should be set at a high level to which the past results indicate to be capable of attainment. Such high standards must frequently result in less variances, which are constant reminders of the improvement still to be made. These may serve as an incentive to greater efforts. While setting up a level of standard, the factors of efficient working under existing conditions should also be taken into consideration.

(b) *Identification of Key factors* : When the attainable budget level is determined, the next important step is to identify the key factors that can influence the budgetary programme with respect to the general policy of the enterprise. The budget of a particular organisation is influenced by certain factors which play a very crucial and decisive role in its development and implementation. These factors may be different for different organisations as per their location, nature of business, availability of resources, marketing structure, government policies in regards to that and priorities fixed by the top management.

(c) *Outlining of the budget* : The budget preparation starts with the preliminary indications of the Budget Committee regarding the broad outline of the plan for the period under review. Thereafter the committee obtains the proposals of all important sections of the organisation with the co-ordination of sectional heads. These proposals should be prepared in the light of set goals and should be a realistic one. It is important that there should be no ambiguity regarding the budgetary goals and provisions between the budget authorities and the persons who are responsible to carry out the budget programme. "It is important to ensure that the scheme of budgetary control is properly explained to each person concerned with its operation in a clear way. During the currency of the scheme full liaison should be maintained between the Budget Committee and the persons responsible for implementing departmental policies."[8] After a formal discussion, the preliminary budget is prepared for each section. It is essential that this preliminary work should be completed early enough to make the final budget to be agreed at the required date which may be a month or two months before the budget comes into operation.

The sectional budget should be a provisional and flexible one as it may be incompatible with other sectional budgets and it may require certain modifications with respect to them. For example :

(a) The budgeted profit may not be acceptable and the sales budget may be altered by an increase in selling price.

(b) The cash budget may indicate that the cash requirements are too much and remedies may be applied, such as a reduction in the purchasing budget, by allowing inventories to be reduced and a reduction in the capital expenditure budget by postponing certain capital projects.

In the course of co-ordinating the sectional budgets, it may be to referred back to the concerned responsibility centres for decisions on matters of doubt or dispute, and the final coordinated budget is normally submitted to this committee for formal approval.

(d) *Budget Finalisation* : When the sectional budgets are approved by the Budget committee, the general budget is finalised by comprising all sectional budgets. This general budget is also called master budget. The general budget is co-ordinated with the sectional budgets in the light of general policies of the enterprise. The general budget is prepared mainly in two parts, one for revenue expenditures and the other for capital expenditures.

(e) *Operation of the Budget* : When the general budget of the business organisation is finalised, the next step is the

8. An introduction to budgetary control, *Standard Costing, Material Control and Production Control*, Published by the Institute of Cost & Works Accountants, London, p. 17.

budget operation with respect to the set goals. Though the ultimate responsibility of budget administration is of the Budget Committee but practically it is mainly a guiding body. The main responsibility of budget operation is assigned to the Sectional Heads who are held responsible to do the assigned work of their respective sections in the light of planned goals. The overall co-ordination is made by the Budget committee in regards to the work performed by the various responsibility centres as the performance of one section can be supplemented with the performance of other sections. Hence, for the successful operation of the budget, it is imperative for all personnel concerned to be fully involved in carrying out the assigned duties.

(f) *Monitoring of the Budget* : The most important aspect of budgeting-process is the monitoring of the budget because only through this the desired goals can be obtained. In this regard, the periodic statements should be prepared comparing the budgetary provisions and actual results and showing the variance between them. To make it more effective, it is essential that such comparative statements be prepared frequently and promptly and the accounting system be organised accordingly. The frequency of these statements as suggested with regard to the period of budget should be largely determined by the requirements of the persons exercising control and cost of frequent preparation of such statements. The budget and actual comparison-statement should be designed so as to place an emphasis on the reasons for the variances. The variances can be analysed on the following points :

(i) **Price Variance** which arises due to payment of higher or lower prices than the standards.

(ii) **Volume Variance** which is a gain or loss due to the volume of business being higher or lower than the standards.

(iii) **Revision Variance** which is the measure of the

effect of revisions to the budget in respect of changed conditions.

(iv) **Methods Variance** which is gain or loss from the use of methods other than those laid down as standards for the product.

(v) **Controllable Variance** which is the gain or loss due to success or failure of the departmental Manager in controlling that expenditure for which he is responsible. This variance may be further analysed according to :

Material Usage Efficiency

Labour Efficiency

Wage and Rate, etc.

Budget and actual comparison statement can be more effective when they are supplemented by explanatory notes, drawing attention to the more significant features of the results and providing explanation not readily apparent in the figures of the statement.

(g) *Corrective Measures* : On the basis of careful consideration of the result shown by the budget and actual comparison statement, decisions for corrective measures should be taken with regard to deviations where the budgeted standards are not achieved. If the budget has been exceeded by an appreciable margin, the real cause for such occurrence should be identified and careful consideration be made for their implications. If the introduction of improvement in methods could not have been anticipated initially and the policies upon which the budget is based, become totally impractical or irrelevant; the substitute budget may be developed in place of the original one.

Essentials of Success of Budgeting

Effective implementation of the management process is essential to achieve the planned goals. Fundamentals of budgeting are key elements for the effective implementation of the management process in reasonable complex efforts. These represent the desirable management orientations, activities and approaches necessary for proficient and sophisticated application of budgeting. The important fundamentals of budgeting are :

(i) Managerial involvement and commitment

(ii) Organisational adaptation

(iii) Responsibility accounting

(iv) Full communication

(v) Realistic expectation

(vi) Budget education

(vii) Time dimension

(viii) Flexible application

(ix) Motivation

(x) Followup.

(i) *Managerial Involvement and Commitment* : Full support of each member of management is essential for the success of budgeting programme. Managerial involvement entails managerial support confidence, participation and performance orientation. In order to engage managerial forces efficiently in budgeting-process, all levels of management, specially top management, must understand the nature and characteristics of budgeting and be convinced as to which particular approach is preferable in a given situation.

Management should also be willing to devote the effort required to make it operative with a view to supporting the programme fully. They should also view the results of the planning process as per the commitments. Stating the involvement of top management required in budgeting, Mr. Welsch states, "Managerial involvement and commitment in a profit planning and control programme is directly related to the confidence that top management has in its ability to influence the future course of certain events significantly and hence the success of the enterprise."[9]

In harmony with this confidence, the management must clearly perceive its duty to plan the future with reasonable

9. Welsch Glenn. *op. cit.*, p. 31.

accuracy and should be convinced with the logic that realistic objectives and goals can be developed in advance. Alongwith this, management should be willing to make firm commitment to plan on a continuing basis. Management should recognise the individuals having administrative responsibilities tending to tie their own success to that of the enterprise so that they would be more aggressive to attain realistic and known objectives, particularly if they are permitted to participate in a meaningful way in developing these objectives.

The idea of participation in budgeting by all level of management entails a behavioural sophistication that a better managed enterprise now recognises. Each manager in the enterprise should expect to carry out assigned responsibilities in every respect, *i.e.*, participation in developing plans for his responsibility centre implementing those plans and exercising own control in their attainment.

For the development of realistic plan for each responsibility centre as well as for the entire entity, the proposal should come up from the lower level. The plan proposals received from the subordinates should be discussed and carefully analysed by the management. Any variation in respect of objectives, goals and standard suggested by the supervisors of lower level must be discussed, then only a definite decision should be taken.

Responsibility for providing the decisions encompassed by the planning process rests squarely on the line executives. In this manner the budgets are viewed as their own and there will be no basis to say that objectives and budget allowances are not fair or realistic.

Thus, it is very important that those line executives, who are responsible to operate the plan in order to achieve the set standards and goals, should be deeply involved in providing the planning decisional inputs for their respective responsibility centres. This procedure makes possible effective implementation of the participation principle in management. Showing the importance of managerial involvement and commitment, Mr. Miller states.... "participation tends to increase commitment, commitment tends to higher motivation, motivation which is job-oriented tends to make managers, work harder and productively and hard and more productive work by managers tends to enhance the company's prosperity."[10]

(ii) *Organisational Adaptation* : A sound organisational structure is a must for the successful operation of budgeting in an enterprise. The purpose of organisational structure and the assignment of the authority is to establish a framework within which enterprise objectives may be attained in a co-ordinated and effective manner on a continuing basis. The scope and inter-relationship of the responsibilities of each individual manager should be defined. The essence of this notion has been stated by Mr. Welsch as.... "viewed internally with respect to the enterprise, responsibility may be defined as the obligation of a subordinate to perform assigned and implied duties. The essence of responsibility is, then obligation. Responsibility has no meaning except as applied to a person : a building, a machine or an animal can not be held responsible."[11] The performance of each individual should be evaluated with respect to the responsibility assigned to them.

Mr. Pandey further adds : "In absence of clearcut assignment of authorities and responsibilities, either the managers will not be held accountable or they will be held accountable for those activities for which they have no responsibility."[12] Such problems arise almost in all enterprises except in very small units. This problem can be solved by dividing an organisation into various sub-units or responsibility centres. Each sub-unit is put under the control of a manager who is assigned specific authority and responsibility to operate that sub-unit. Some important responsibility centres classified on the basis of extent of responsibility can be cost centre, profit centre and investment centre. Through these responsibility centres planned goals are attained by implementing plans and controlling them efficiently.

---

10. Ernest, C. Miller, *Objectives and Standards : An Approach to Planning & Control*, A.M.A. Research Study, 74, New York, Americal Management Association, Inc.

11. Weksch Glenn, *op. cit.*, p. 33.

12. Pandey, I.M., *Financial Management,* Vikash Publishing House Pvt. Ltd., New Delhi, 79, p. 471.

Thus, budgeting must be tailored to the organisational sub-units and the related structural characteristics of the enterprise.

(iii) *Responsibility Accounting* : It includes the controlling of costs at the point incurred. It means that managers of all levels have to be brought into the framework of budgetary control.

In order to set up a sound budgetary system, the development of responsibility accounting is essential. Plans are based on realistic data which are generated by the accounting systems and controlling is made by comparing the actual result with the budgetary provisions. Effective control is a must to achieve the pre-determined goals, which is only possible, when accounting system is developed on a responsibility line that can generate required authentic data. If the data are not available as per the requirement of responsibility centres, the budgeting cannot be operated successfully. So the accounting system must be built around the responsibility structure of the enterprise that can generate relevant data for effective operation of budgeting.

The cost accounting plays a very important role in budgetary control through applying the responsibility accounting. The traditional approach of cost accounting was only to determine the cost of goods produced but the responsibility accounting gives much more emphasis on generating relevant data for planning and control through which only the budgeting can be operated effectively.

(iv) *Full Communication* : Communication is an interchange of thought or information to bring about a mutual understanding between two or more parties. The primary responsibility of management is to develop objectives and plans for the organisation and then to devise ways and means to fulfil the planned goals. The set objectives can be achieved only by the united efforts which require effective communication among all the persons engaged in operating those plans.

The effective communication does not only make people aware of the organisational goals and plans but also modifies their behavioural outlook that can give them tremendous results. Mr. Welsch viewed .... "Management is implemented through communication, the means by which behaviour is affected, modified and energised."[13]

The decision-making process of management rests upon the effective communication up to a greater extent, If the person to whom the matter is communicated, understands its meaning clearly, he can take an idea immediately to implement it successfully. To communicate the adequate information successfully, there must be three primary flows of information in the organisation. These are downward communication, upward communication and lateral communication.

Budgeting-practices, resting upon a sound foundation of communication, provide important avenues to enhance effective communication. Fundamentally these relate to the process of developing enterprise objectives, specification of goals, the development of budget, reporting and the follow-up activities related to performance evaluation for each responsibility centre. Effective communication is a must for effective planning and control so that both the executives and subordinates have the same understanding of responsibility and goals.

(v) *Realistic Expectations* : Budgeting can be operated successfully and efficiently only when the management functions with realistic expectation and its objectives should represent "expected actual." It should neither have undue conservation nor irrational optimism. To be realistic, management expectations must be related : (i) to their specific time dimensions and (ii) to an assumed external and internal environment that will prevail during that time span.

The goals should be set with such expectations which are possible to attain practically. Near impossible goals should be discouraged. On the other hand, the goals set so low as not to require any serious effort, will provide no motivation. "Enterprise objectives and specific budget goals in order to constitute realistic expectations must represent a real challenge to the manager and to the operational units."[14]

Thus, the policies should be framed in such a way by the top

13. Welsch Glenn, *op. cit.*, p. 37.

14. Welsch Glenn, *op. cit.*, p. 39.

management that can provide maximum motivation to the individual manager, operational units and the overall enterprise to excel. These realistic expectations must be defined with respect to the size of organisation, working conditions, availability of resources, capacity, sophistication of the management at all levels, nature of operations and the psychological factors.

(vi) *Budget Education* : The success of the profit planning and control depends upon the active participation of all the personnels of an enterprise. This is possible only when they clearly understand the budgeting-technique followed in the organisation. For this they should be educated with all the aspects of budgeting, to set goals and guidelines for effective implementation of the budget.

In developing planned objectives through managerial participation, a problem arises frequently which is called 'padding the budget.' This can be explained by the examples given below :

1. Sales budget estimates are understated — to protect ourselves and exceeding the sales budget certainly cannot be criticised.
2. Overestimating expenses — so we will have plenty of money and spending less than the budgetary provisions looks good to the management.
3. Requisitioning more cash than needed — so that we would not have to ask for more and if we turn some back, it will look good.

To minimise the above mentioned natural tendencies, enlightened management has to develop effective approaches. The continuous and effective budget education aimed at developing positive attitudes towards planning and control, can be helpful to solve these problems concerned with psychological phenomena.

The objectives of the budget education programme should be :

(i) To communicate the policies and intentions of the top management relating to the planning and control programme to all responsibility centres;

(ii) To develop the positive attitudes so that each and every individual involved in the budget operation should identify the success of the organisation with his own success and

(iii) To issue the instructions in such a way that they can contribute to the effective performance of the managerial tasks of each individual.

(vii) *Time Dimension* : The budgeting-programme cannot be carried out successfully in any organisation until and unless due consideration is made to the time factor. "Effective implementation of the profit planning and control concept requires that the management of the enterprise establish a definite time dimension for certain type of decision."[15]

There are two important phases of time that require special attention of the planners. One is concerned with the concept of planning horizons and the other is the timing of planning activities. Planning horizons refer to that period of time for which management makes plan in a particular situation.

The period of time for the budget should be decided on the basis of the nature of the business. The budgets for the industries which are influenced by short period changes in consumer demand, require a different approach from the one found in the industries involving long term expenditure with relatively little change in product features. "The period of time covered by a budget, and the resulting comparative statement of actual and budgeted expenditure should be largely determined by the requirements and the outlook of the person whose activities it plans."[16] To obtain full benefit from budgetary control, it is also necessary that the main budget should be supplemented by short period budgets. *For example*, the control of the cash position may require the monthly budgeting of the requirement and receipts of cash.

A successful Manager is one, who does not rest upon the last minute-decisions to achieve organisational goals, who anticipates

15. Welsch Glenn, *op. cit.*, p. 41.

16. *An Introduction to Budgetary Control, Standard costing, Material Control and Production Control*, Published by the Institute of cost & works Accountants, London, p. 17.

major promotional decisions through an intergraded and systematic approach. This systematic approach can be evolved smoothly by the operation of budgeting programmes.

The timing of planning is another important factor that requires careful attention for the successful operation of budgeting in an enterprise. There should be a definite time schedule for intimating and completing the planning process. Managerial planning should be viewed as a continuous process at all levels of management that can be carried out successfully only when they have a definite planning calendar. When they have a definite time schedule, they can assess, re-assess, modify the plans accordingly and can take appropriate decisions for day-to-day affairs. Besides the above-mentioned phases, the time dimension is equally important for the control function of management. To perform the control function effectively in an enterprise, the performance report should be prepared on a monthly, weekly and daily basis as and when required. Follow-up actions must be implemented in time.

(viii) *Flexible Application* : The principle of flexibility should be followed essentially at the time of budget operation. The conditions prevailing at the time of the development of budget may change during its operation due to various factors. To control such variations in the situation, the provisions should be chalked out, in advance, then only it can be implemented effectively.

The principle of flexibility becomes more important while controlling the cost in which the variations can occur frequently. In regard to the need of the flexible application of budget, Mr. Welsch states..... 'The budget not be viewed as a strategic jacket and to emphasise that the planning and control approach to management does not constrain the management in seizing all opportunities, whether planned for or not, that will accrue to the economic well-being of the enterprise.'

Initial budgetary provisions must be revised in accordance with the changed conditions and actual performance should be compared with the revised budgetary provisions for the realistic evaluation of performance. The budgeting approach should anticipate expectations, adjustments and re-plan as situation evolves.

(ix) *Motivation* : Today an organisation is facing a serious psychological problem of unpredictable behaviour in regard to response by the individual or group concerned. The motivation of human resources through dynamic leadership is the key point for the success of management. A serious thought and careful attention of the management is needed to deal with the behavioural aspect. These behavioural problems can be brought into sharp focus by effective application of budgeting programme effectively.

The satisfaction, that one gets from accomplishment of the goals and from being a participant in activities, that appears relevant to him, becomes much more important for him than any monetary reward. It tends towards the goal orientation much more. "Realistic goals established through meaningful participation tends to raise the aspiration level of the entire management in a firm."[17] The budgeting provides a means to resolve the goal orientation problem in an enterprise by involving all level of management effectively in developing the goals, related policies and their implementation. Sometimes pressure is also required to motivate the concerned personnels on a continuing basis. Certain aspects of budgeting-practices are used as extreme pressure devices to motivate people towards greater efforts.

One important aspect of behavioural view point is that there must be a fair evaluation of individuals for their outstanding performance or sub-standard performance and it should be recognised and identified by the management. "The essential obligations of an enlightened management are to define the potentialities, to create a working atmosphere in which men will want to strive towards them and to attract the kind of man who can and will participate in such a growth process."[18]

The dignity of the individual is important in the process of management. The proper budgeting-system entails a procedure for careful evaluation of planning capabilities and performance of the managers. Through the performance reports and observations,

---

17. Andrew, C. Stedry, *Budget conrol and cost Behaviour,* (Englewood Cliffs, N.J., Prentice Hall, 1960), Chapter-13.

18. Saul, G. Gellerman, *People, Problems and Profit : The Use of Psychology in Management,* (New York : McGraw-Hill Book Co., Inc., 1960), p. 249.

the persons of high competence are recognised and of low competence are identified. This potential for capable evaluation of management potentials of each individual, certainly possesses behavioural implications of consequence.

(x) *Follow up* : Effective control can be exercised only when the performance of each responsibility centre is evaluated regularly in the light of the budgetary provisions. The actual result should be compared with the budgetary standards at the regular time intervals. In the evaluation process, the outstanding performance or sub-standard performance of the group or any individual should be noticed. The special recognition should be made for the outstanding performance and the corrective measures should be taken for substandard performance.

The time factor is more important in regard to follow up action. When the variance analysis is completed, the reasons responsible for any deviation should be identified and the corrective measures should be taken to root-out the cause within a stipulated time period. Again to measure the effects of corrective measures, an evaluation of performance should be made. As the situations change due to influence of various factors, it is not always possible to achieve the planned goals. These must be replanned according to the changed situation. Thus, the evaluation of performance and follow up action in proper time must be exercised within a reasonable time.

Importance of Budgeting

In recent years, the budgeting has been accorded a unique and relevant role especially in accomplishing the management process with maximum long range effectiveness. The modern management has found that it must chart its course in advance and use appropriate techniques to assure effective co-ordination and control operations in order to keep pace with the cut-throat competition. As a consequence, the approach of profit planning and control has found a wide essential acceptance at present.

The main thrust of budgeting goes to the very heart of managing the decision-making process. For the long range success, the stream of managerial decisions must generate plans and actions to provide the essential inflows, that are necessary to support the planned outflows of the enterprise to ensure the earning of realistic profit and return on investment. It gives absolute confidence to the management to establish realistic objectives for the enterprise.

Thus, the effective application of budgeting makes it possible for the management to feel the pulse of the enterprise throughout the year. More specifically, the satisfactory or unsatisfactory progress towards the overall as well as more specific goals of the enterprise can be known. It makes the task of managing more systematic, more effective, and more rewarding. It can be applied so as to impart a high degree of flexibility in management process.

The application of budgeting is important to assess the material requirement for a long period ahead enabling favourable purchase terms. Production process can be operated with all economies such as the reduction in time, specialisation of plants, tools and labour force resulting in higher output per man hours or machine hours. Through the controlling aspect of budgeting, management can be able to measure the deviations of actual results from budgetary standards from time to time. The factors, responsible for such deviations, can be identified, and corrective measures can be taken within an appropriate time and ultimately the desired results can be obtained as per the predetermined objectives.

The Use of Budgeting

Budgeting is mainly used for the following purposes :

(i) To define the objectives of the organisation as a whole.

(ii) To define the results to be achieved by departments and personnel thereof for the purpose of realising the organisational objectives.

(iii) To reveal the extent by which actual results have exceeded or failed to reach the defined objectives.

(iv) To measure the magnitude of variances and establish the causes of variations as a basis of executive action to correct adverse trends or secure benefits from favourable conditions.

(v) To secure the most economical use of the factors of production.

(vi) To provide a measure of the efficiency with which the activities of the organisation have been co-ordinated.

(vii) To provide a basis for future policy and if required, revision of current policy.

(viii) To facilitate a centralised control in circumstances of decentralised activity.

(ix) To facilitate stabilisation of industrial or other activities in conditions subject to seasonal or other cyclical influences.

Besides the above mentioned main uses, there are also some secondary uses of the budgeting as given below :

(i) To establish the conditions precedent to the establishment of standard costs;

(ii) To provide a basis of internal audit by regular examination of departmental results;

(iii) To provide a basis for forms of incentive remuneration related to the results expected in a period of time and

(iv) Lastly, to act as an instrument of management policy whereby the extension of the schemes to lower level management to enable the top management to decentralise responsibility and centralise control.

Historical Evolution of Budgeting

The Consolidated Fund Act, 1787 was the first important milestone in the history of budget because it considered budget as a comprehensive financial statement of government activities for facilitating accountability of public fund.

The 'Forecasting', an important element of budgeting-technique was used in Egypt by Joseph when he "budgeted to cover the expected supply and demand for corn and for related activities."[19] Though the forecasting did not imply the same thing as budgeting, it gave a clearway for the development of budgeting-technique.

19. Puri, Y.P., "Budgeting — Government Business & Performance", *Lok Udyog*, August, 1973.

In modern sense, the first step towards budgeting was started in Great Britain in the 18th century by passing the Exchequer and Audit Department Act, 1866 by the Parliament. This Act was passed to make the provisions for collecting money through taxes for government expenditures. Initially the 'Budget' was used to collect money and to indicate how it was to be spent.

The reference of budgetary control in the field of industry was made by S.H. Burnell, first time in 1911 in Britain and it was further developed in the article "The Planning of Finance" by H.J. Jenkins, published in the Cost Accountant in August, 1922. But the budgetary control was firmly established when the Ninth National Cost Conference was held in October, 1930. The members of the Institute of Cost and Works Accountants emphasised the development of budgetary control. The term "Budgetary Control" alleged by H.G. Jenkins, "seems to have caught the fancy of the business organisation".

Though the concept of 'budget' and 'budgeting' evolved properly in the 19th century, in the last fifty years the dynamic changes took place in its approach and technique. During this, the budget became an important instrument of policy which is now employed to stimulate economic growth. to control inflation and even to use selective measures in particular geographic areas "From being a purely financial device, the budget has become a tool of government, just as budgetary control is a tool of management."[20] Use of standard cost in place of actual cost for profit planning and control gave new dimensions to its development. During this phase, budgeting grew out of the reform movement. Subsequently, the emergence of Line Item Budgeting, Performance Budgeting, Planning Programme Budgeting and Zero Base Budgeting made it the most effective tool of modern management practices. A brief description of these is given below :

Line Item Budgeting. The Line Item Budgeting is also known as 'Object Account Budget.' It enumerates estimated expenditure classified on the basis of 'typed and quantity' for a

---

20. See D. Solomons (ed.) *Studies in Costing*, Sweeta Maxwell, London, 1952, p. 45.

particular period usually for one year. In this the organisational budget is formulated for the various units, departments, sections and divisions separately and various types of expenditures are listed categorically.

The basic purpose of this kind of budgeting is to control the expenditures and to monitor the fiscal resources in such a way as to ensure the proper utilisation of the public fund. Thus, it encourages management to balance the budget and review it regularly in accordance with the proceedings of the financial affairs of the organisation. Though it provides for a short range fiscal control effectively, this type of budgeting has several inherent limitations which are as follows :

- (i) It does not prove to be too useful for a long range planning.
- (ii) It lacks the comparative analysis of actual results with the planned objectives.
- (iii) New appropriations are made on the basis of the previous year budget.
- (iv) It creates conflicts among the various units of the organisation for available funds.
- (v) Any duplication, redundant activities and tasks are hard to detect.
- (vi) It encourages 'management by crisis', because there is a tendency to concentrate only on the most pressing demands thereby avoiding activities whose fiscal effects cannot be seen immediately.

Performance Budgeting

The second stage of the development budgeting is performance budgeting which was emphasised by Hoover Commission appointed by the U.S. Government in 1949. It lays emphasis on accomplishment rather than on the means of accomplishment. The performance budgeting is a technique that chalks out a plan of what to do and to what extent, at what cost and with what results. "In performance budgeting.... the physical and financial aspects of each programme and activity are correlated by establishing relationship between output and related inputs."[21]

In India, the approach of performance budgeting was made in 1973. Before that the attempt to measure the physical performance and the evaluation of expenditure with respect to actual results was never considered by the business organisations in India.

Though the approach of performance budgeting gives a thorough idea about the allocation of funds and their uses to the planners, there are certain limitations to it. This approach does not fix the priorities for the budgeting programme and also fails to recognise the alternative means through which it can be implemented to achieve set goals. Use of standard costing and responsibility accounting techniques can make it more result oriented.

Planning Programming Budgeting

Planning Programming Budgeting is also known as Programme Budgeting. This is the third important phase of development in budgeting technique in which more attention is given to the aspects of the functions, objectives, effectiveness and the outcome. The planning programming system of budgeting has concentrated on the development of an allocative process that can evaluate competitive claims for government expenditures.

The formal use of this was initiated first time in 1961 in the Defence Department of the United States and it was extended to all other external agencies in 1965 at the directive of the then U.S. President. It was intended to encompass a long-range framework of planning for the development of a sound budgeting that could relate programmes to objectives and could also evaluate the costs and benefits of alternative programmes. It was also aimed at the long term benefits and effectiveness of current strategies and programmes. The method was developed to promote the analysis of key policy matters of the business organisation to facilitate a technique to identify the trade offs among programmes aimed at similar objectives. It could translate the strategic goals into time phased requirement of material and human beings.

21. Prem Chand, A., *Performance Budgeting*, Academic Books, Bombay, 1969.

The very sad part of the planning programming budgeting was that it totally failed in the U.S.A. and consequently was abandoned in 1971. The basic reasons of its failure were the over emphasis on analysis held out as panacea to all federal government problems, unavailability of instant solutions, faulty implementation of strategy, lack of properly trained staff, undeveloped techniques, etc.

Zero Base Budgeting

The concept of Zero Base Budgeting originated in 1924 when E. Hilto Yound had emphasised the need for annual rejustification of budget programme. But it was Mr. Peter A. Pyhrr who designed its logical framework and implemented in successfully in the private industry in 1969 when he was working as a Staff Control Manager in Texas Instruments USA. Pyhre reviewed a speech given by Dr. Arthur F. Burns proposing "that all government agency programmes be reviewed entirely each year and claiming that substantial cost savings could be realized from the comprehensive review."[22]

Zero Base Budgeting is an operating planning and budgeting which requires each manager to justify his entire budget request of each period in detail from Zero Base. Each manager states why he should spend any money at all. This approach requires that all activities be identified as "decision packages" which will be evaluated by systematic analysis and ranked in order of importance. Thus, the process requires managers to justify an entire budget request rather than just the incremental changes from the previous year's budget. A Typical Zero Base Budgeting would involve several steps as explained below :

1. Identification of Decision Units

A decision unit is a distinctive entity within an organisation for which a budget request is prepared. Decision units can revolve round cost centres, projects, programmes, budget units or any other entities which can be analysed and for which budget decision must be made.

---

22. Phyhrr, A Peter, *Zero Base Budgeting — A Practical Management Tool for Evoluating Expenses*, John Wiley & Sons, New York, 1973.

2. Formulation of Decision Packages

The decision unit manager formulates in order of importance a list of decision packages, the total value of which equals the value of the budget request for the concerned unit. Each decision package consists of an clearly identifiable set of services, activities or expenditures. A decision unit package should contain : (a) an identification of the decision package as a decision unit increment, (b) a description of the services to be provided or activities to be performed if the package is funded, (c) the resource requirements of the package and their costs, (d) a quantitative expression of work load output, (e) an evaluation of the effects of changes if the package is not funded.

A minimum level decision package is initially prepared representing the activity programme and its fund levels below which it is not feasible to continue the decision unit because no constructive contribution can be made towards fulfilling the programme objectives. This package normally has a requested funding level significantly lower than the previous year's budget. Once a minimum level decision package has been identified, the manager can propose additional packages which represent additional levels of activity and funding for the unit. The total of all the units decision packages equals the budget proposals of an enterprise.

3. Ranking

In the Zero Base Budgeting, ranking plays a key role in selecting the most effective decision package for funding. The ranking facilitates management with a technique to allocate budget resources. It requires managers to assign priorities to budget increments with respect to its objectives and the limit of amount to be spent on it.

The decision packages are ranked in order of decreasing benefits to the organisational decision unit. This process fixes priorities on the basis of function described in the decision packages. The increments developed by decision unit Manager provide the basic information from which higher level managers allocate critical resources to high priority activities.

The initial ranking of decision packages occurs at the

organisational level where the analysis is developed to allow each manager to evaluate their efficiency in regards to their ability to make trade-offs between level of services seeking to optimise the return on expenditures. This ranking is reviewed at the higher level of the organisation and used as a guide for merging those rankings. In the process of ranking, all packages (projects/programmes) are evaluated from various aspects such as economic aspect or return on investment, costs savings aspect, net present value, discounted cash flow, cost benefits ratio and pay back period, etc.

Advantages of Zero Base Budgeting

The benefits of Zero Base Budgeting can be discussed as under :

(i) Helpful in developing more logical and systematic approach to budget justification;

(ii) Greater participation of the line managers in the budget process;

(iii) Provides more flexible budget tool that facilitates policy review and impact on trade-off analysis;

(iv) Considers alternative means of performing the same job;

(v) Gives focus on management process of analysis and decision-making;

(vi) Improves the planning process;

(vii) Requires each budget request to be justified which makes it more goal oriented;

(viii) Permits trade-offs within the departments;

(ix) Relates costs and benefits of programmes which enable decision-makers to follow-up on cost and Performance and

(x) Reduces the duplication of staff efforts.

Though the Zero Base Budgeting has several benefits, some coveat need to be noted in this regard :

(1) Developments have shown Zero Base Budgeting to be something of a misnomer. Budgeting remains largely an incremental process. This is primarily due to the limits of human information

processing. What has evolved is rather a zero-base review or perhaps more likely an 80 per cent base review with only 20 per cent of the budget subject to complete review.

(2) There are some evidences that could have destabilising effect within an organisation. Paradoxically this could occur when an organisation has proved to be more forward looking into management development programmes by introducing such schemes as Management by Objectives. The 'decoupling' cost may be high as staff move from one technique to another.

(3) While there are strategies available to moderate the impact of Zero Base Budgeting, there is some evidence of costing their relevance costing additional resources for implementation. *For example*, extensive computing resources would appear to be a pre-requisite for any attempt to implement 'Pure' Zero Base Budgeting in a comprehensive and sustained manner in an organisation of any significant size.

The basic problems involved in Zero Base Budgeting can be outlined as below :

(i) Difficulty in evaluating different or dissimilar functional 'decision package';

(ii) More time and effort required in analysis of the decision packages;

(iii) Difficulty in ranking of large number of decision packages;

(iv) More administrative and communicative efforts are required;

(v) Difficult to obtain cost/performance information;

(vi) Bridging the gap between theory and practice is difficult;

(vii) The resistance to change of individual working with system;

(viii) Difficulty in the development of decision packages on the line of various criteria or aspects;

(ix) Managers are threatened by Zero Base Budgeting systems.

3

Budgeting — Classification of Budgets

The entire budgetary system of an organisation for a defined period is represented by a master budget which is detailed in subsidiary budgets. The classification of budget has been made by various authorities on different grounds but mainly it can be classified on the basis of coverage, capacity conditions and periods. "Budgets can be classified by (a) the coverage they encompass, (b) the capacity to which they are related, (c) the conditions on which they are based and (d) the period which they cover."[1]

On the basis of this most acceptable classification given by Prof. Swaminathan, a master chart showing the budget classification can be outlined as below :

Budget-Classification

- On the basis of coverage
  - Functional Budgets
  - Master Budget
- On the basis of capacity
  - Fixed Budget
  - Flexible Budget
- On the basis of conditions
  - Basic Budget
  - Current Budget
- On the basis of periods
  - Long-term Budget
  - Short-term Budget

Budget-Classification on the Basis of Coverage

The master chart of budget-classification shows that the most important classification of budgets is coverage-based classification that incorporates the functional budgets and the master budget.

1. Swaminathan, L., *Lectures on Costing*, 1968, p. 338.

Functional Budgets

The budgets prepared for each important functional aspect of an organisation are called functional budgets. They may be prepared mainly for the following heads :

(i) Sales Budget

(ii) Production Budget

(iii) Plant Utilization Budget

(iv) Production Cost Budget :

Purchase Budget

Works Overheads Budget

Personnel Budget

(v) Selling and Distribution Cost Budget

(vi) Research and Development Budget

(vii) Office and Administration Budget

(viii) Capital Expenditures Budget

(ix) Cash Budget

A brief description of the functional budgets is given below :

Sales Budget

Sale is the fundamental aspect of all other functions of the enterprise.

"Unless a realistic planning and control of this aspect is made, no other elements of profit plans can be piltered with reality. The sales plan is the foundation for periodic planning in the firm, because all other enterprise planning is built on it."[2] The primary source of cash is sales, the capital additions needed the amount of expenses to be planned, the manpower requirements, the production level and other important operational aspects depend on the volume of sale.

The sales budget is a forecast of total sales expressed in both in terms of money and quantities. A periodic plan for sales

2. Welsch, Glenn, A., *Budgeting Profit Planning and Control*, p. 139.

volume is prepared by assessing the total number of units of each group of products to be sold and the money value of the budgeted unit is also ascertained. In harmony with the comprehensive profits-plan, an integrated long-term and short-term sales plan must be developed. Long-term sales-plans are developed normally as annual amount, whereas the short-term sales-plans are developed for the year by quarterly or monthly break up. In the long-run sales-plan, broad groupings of products should be made with the sophisticated analysis of further potentials of the marketing, population changes, projection of the industry as well as the company concerned. The short-term plan comprises a detailed plan for each major product and for groupings of minor products which are normally developed in terms of physical units as well as monetary terms

The primary objective of a sales-plan is to express the best judgment of the management on potential sales revenues. These judgements should be based upon the (i) present knowledge of the company; (ii) the environments, (iii) the impact on the firm of enterprise objective and (iv) long-run and short-run managerial strategies.

The important components that should be generalised for the foundation of comprehensive sales planning are (i) enterprise objectives, (ii) enterprise strategies (iii) sales forecastings.

Enterprise objectives provide the broad goals around which the sales plan is developed while managerial strategies provide a basis for judgements of the impact of the aggressive company actions and the sales forecasts provide a technical projection of the customers-demand. The sales forecasting is the most important tool of the sales budget........ "Nevertheless, correct forecasting of sales is essential as the entire basis of profit planning on this forecasts."[3] The external factors like government policy, trade cycle, purchasing capacity and change in habits of buyers, influence the sales forecasting deeply. Besides sales trends, the sales-prices, seasonal products, incoming of new products and

3. Prasad, N.K., *Principles and Practices of Cost Accounting*, 1977, pp. 16-21.

desired amount of profit are some of the internal factors that also influence the sales forecasting. The internal and external factors should be microscopically analysed for correct and realistic forecasting of sales.

Sales-forecasting is the foundation of quantification of the entire business-plan. The sales-forecasting is made by the Chief Sales Officer after considering the following factors :

(i) Past Sales Volume,

(ii) General Economic and industrial conditions,

(iii) Relationship of sales to economic indicators such as gross national product, personal income, employment, prices and industrial production,

(iv) Relative product profitability,

(v) Market Research Studies,

(vi) Pricing policies,

(vii) Advertising and other promotion,

(viii) Quality of sale force,

(ix) Competition,

(x) Seasonal variation,

(xi) Production Capacity,

(xii) Long-run sales-trends for various products.

There are several methods of sales-forecasting and each acts as a check on the other. The following methods of sales forecasting are usually combined in some fashion that is suitable for a specific company :

(1) **Sales-Prediction by sales Personnel.** The responsible persons for sale should play an active role in the formulation of sales budget. The budget data should flow from the individual sales man to the Chief Sales Officer "A valuable benefit from the budgeting process is the holding of discussions which generally result in adjustments and which tend to broaden participants thinking."[4] Thus, sales forecasts by the selling staff serve as an

4. Charles, T. Horngren, *Cost Accounting — Managerial Emphasis*, Prentice Hall of India Pvt. Ltd., New Delhi, 1976, p. 139.

incentive for their involvement in budgeting process. But sometimes the figures collected by the staff may be influenced by personal prejudices so the figures should be analysed continuously so that over-optimism or the undue estimate of the sales may be prevented.

(2) **Past Sales Figures and Trends.** The compiler of the sales budget should take into consideration of graphs regarding past sales and the general sales trends. Previous sales volumes are usually the spring boar for sales predictions. Sales Executives should examine historical sales behaviour and relate it to other historical data such as economic indicators, advertising, pricing policies and competitive conditions. Besides these, the growth of market, seasonal fluctuations, trade cycles should also be kept in mind while forecasting the sales figures. These factors should be supplemented by the details of the sales of the previous periods and should be analysed by product area class of consumers, customers and agent. Thus, past records of different factors influencing sale may prove the most reliable guide for future sales.

(3) **Market Research.** To make more reliable forecasting of sales, the sales executives should gather concrete information through market research. Their opinion should not be based only upon the figures but they should have to assess the possibilities of increasing sales volume and to evolve the ways to get it done. The customers-motivation can be evaluated through market research. "Market research tries to find out which of the company's product can be sold in a period and in what quantities at what price and in which market. Such an analysis can be made to assess the potential demands according to customers, territories, salesmen, channels of distribution, size of orders or terms of sales."[5]

(4) **The statistical Analysis.** It is also a useful technique to make a reliable sales-forecasting. The projection of trends and cycles can be made through the correlation analysis between the sales and economic indicators. The more fluctuations in economic

5. Prasad, N.K., *Principles and Practices of Cost Accounting*, 1977, pp. 16-21.

indicators precede fluctuations in the sale of the company also. As the sale of a particular firm is affected by the general trade conditions, a statistical analysis should be made in accordance with these. However, no firm should rely entirely on this approach because too much reliance on statistical evidences may be dangerous due to variations in data.

(5) **Group Analysis.** The sales forecast can also be made by the group-opinion developed through collective discussions. The top managers of various responsibility centres, *i.e.*, production, purchasing, finance and administrative, may project sales by using their experience and knowledge. They can analyse the various trade conditions and factors like material and labour supply position, market competition, long-run sales trends, government policies, advertising and sales promotion, etc.

Although all the above methods for sales forecasting can be useful in their own way, no single method can prove to be perfect in forecasting of sales. A method, which is most effective for a particular firm or company, cannot be equally useful for the others. The conditions may be different as per the characteristics, environment, size, nature of products and time limit. These factors can affect the approach used for the reliable sales forecasting. "Sales budgeting can never be static, the individual company must continuously strive, improve the various techniques, approaches and concepts underlying its particular method of predicting sales."[6]

It is, therefore, essential to use a combined approach of these methods to formulate a realistic sales budget in the light of managerial commitment towards the goal of the enterprise. Accordingly, sales prediction must be adjusted, co-ordinated and synchronised in harmony with the production capacity and other operational aspects of the organisation.

While preparing a sales budget, the following factors should be taken into consideration by the budget authorities :

(1) **Plant Capacity.** One of the primary essentials of a profitable business is to ensure the proper utilisation of plant

---

6. Welsch, Glenn, *op. cit.*, 1976, p. 163.

facilities. It is, therefore, essential that the information as regards to the plant capacity and present utilisation of the capacity for different product groups should be known to prepare a reliable sales budget.

(2) **General Trade Prospects.** The trend of the sales depends largely on the general trade prospects. It is, therefore, essential to take these prospects into consideration while preparing a sales budget for a particular industry. In this regard, valuable informations may be gathered from various financial publication.

(3) **Orders on Hand.** The value of orders on hand may have a considerable weight in determining the value of sales to be budgeted for a particular period, specially in boom periods or where the production is in a very lengthy process. Therefore, orders received must be balanced with the orders delivered.

(4) **Proposed Expansion or discontinuance of products.** Any proposed expansion or discontinuance of product should be taken into consideration while preparing a sales budget. The margin of the profit on each product, the facilities for manufacturing as well as the visualised potential market are the factors that influence this decision.

(5) **Proposed Alteration in Quality and Price.** In preparing the sales budget, the effect of any such adjustment on the volume as well as on the value of sales must not be forgotten. It is often very difficult to determine the price effect on any such alteration. Therefore, careful market research studies may require to be made before making any alteration in this regard so that a reliable sales budget may be prepared.

(6) **Seasonal Fluctuations.** The past experience may be the most reliable guideline in assessing seasonal variations. A determined effort should be made to minimise such variations for the ideal of an even flow of production. In this context, the first consideration should be given to the reasons due to which such fluctuations take place. These can be identified as climatic trade orders effect, change in customs and habits and repercussions of these on allied industries. The effect of these can be minimised by taking steps towards special advertising, special concessions or added

inducements during the off-season. On the production side, the problem might be tackled by the introduction of different supplementary or alternative lines when the demand for the principal products is slack, or by the controlled building up of stocks. But the cost of all such proposals must be set against any expected benefit. Before the final approval of the sales budget, this problem should be settled.

(7) **Potential Market.** A reliable estimate of the potential market for the company's products is essential. It determines the capital required, the building of plants, when extension should be carried out and what sales force and what advertising mode should be employed. The estimates may be based on one man's unrecorded knowledge of a particular trade or by the result of carefully undertaken market research. It should be both for the demand and supply.

(8) **Availability of Material and Labour.** A controlling factor, which sometime arises in drafting the sales budget, may be the availability of materials and labour. The likelihood of obtaining adequate supplies of materials and labour must be fully investigated before drafting the sales budgets. If it is apparent that this factor could limit deliveries, the programme will require to be modified accordingly.

(9) **Trade Cycle.** This is an established phenomenon. The ups and downs can be seen easily but it is very difficult to make an accurate estimate as to when and how far it is going to happen. There are various methods of anticipating the future trend. The ideal for any business would be to find out the trends of some other business or trade of similar nature.

Today political events and government control of external and internal trade and finance play an important role in trade conditions. It would appear advisable to place a great reliance on a detailed consideration of these factors. They affect the current conditions and influence the future more than they are guided by any apparent regular cyclical fluctuation.

(10) **Financial Aspect.** Finance is one of the most important factors that should be taken into consideration while preparing a sales budget. Sales expansion usually involves capital outlay. So

sufficient funds must be made available to finance the operations. A company with a good credit standing or a plentiful supply of capital may not depend much more on the funds raised through sales only. But a small firm or one in which it is difficult to obtain capital, sales budget may require to be kept within the bounds of the financial capacity. Therefore, sales volume should be planned in such a way which can ensure an adequate return on the capital employed.

Keeping in consideration the above important factors, a comprehensive sales budget can be prepared with the following procedure :

(a) A preliminary budget giving total for the principal products groups should be made out from reference to previous experience and general trade products;

(b) Another more detailed budget based on salesman's and agents' reports should be made out for the future;

(c) Both the above should be compared side by side and be modified in the light of the other one after a further investigation.

The central forecasting department of the company develops a tentative sales plan based on market potentials estimated in the light of pricing and inventory policies. The marketing research and forecasting efforts are conducted at the staff level continuously. Simultaneously the sales data of past are obtained and modified in accordance with the projections and recommendations made by the sales personnel. These figures are deeply reviewed by the marketing executives and are compared with the sales forecast developed by the central forecasting group. Finally, it is evaluated and adjusted in the light of broad objectives of the company and enterprise strategies at the level of top management. On the basis of such a reliable sale forecasting a comprehensive sales plan for the budget year is developed with respect to product, area and time period.

This adjusted budget should then be considered in relation to plant capacity, balanced productions and to a proposed extension. Items to be expanded or discontinued should also be taken into account for such adjustments. This revised budget should again be considered in the light of trade conditions and of the policy and other factors enumerated. It may be found worthwhile to make up the budget again by product, by area, by consumer class and should be analysed with respect to balancing each other. Thus, the sales budget is finalised and incorporated in master budget.

The sales budget may be prepared in the following format :

Sales Budget (by Product)
Year ———

Months	Product-I		Product-II		Product-III		Total	
	Quantity	Values	Quantity	Values	Quantity	Values	Quantity	Values
January								
February								
March								
April								
May								
June								
July								
August								
September								
October								
November								
December								
Total								

With the help of the following information, the sales budget of A.B.C. & Company Ltd. for the budget year 1998 can be prepared. The Company sold its X, Y and Z products in four different zones. The budgeted sales figures and actual sales figures for current year are given below :

(I)

Budgeted Sales for (1997)

ZONES	*PRODUCT-X*		*PRODUCT-Y*		*PRODUCT-Z*	
	Units	*Rate per Unit (Rs.)*	*Units*	*Rate per Unit (Rs.)*	*Units*	*Rate per Unit (Rs.)*
NORTH	40,000	20.00	32,000	36.00	60,000	64.00
SOUTH	48,000	20.00	28,000	36.00	40,000	64.00
EAST	20,000	20.00	36,000	36.00	60,000	64.00
WEST	80,000	20.00	40,000	36.00	48,000	64.00
TOTAL	**1,88,000**		**1,36,000**		**2,08,000**	

(II)

Actual Sales for (1997)

ZONES	*PRODUCT-X*		*PRODUCT-Y*		*PRODUCT-Z*	
	Units	*Rate per Unit (Rs.)*	*Units*	*Rate per Unit (Rs.)*	*Units*	*Rate per Unit (Rs.)*
NORTH	48,000	20.00	40,000	36.00	52,000	64.00
SOUTH	40,000	20.00	32,000	36.00	36,000	64.00
EAST	32,000	20.00	28,000	36.00	56,000	64.00
WEST	80,000	20.00	32,000	36.00	60,000	64.00
TOTAL	**2,00,000**		**1,32,000**		**2,04,000**	

Besides these information, the other important information have also been gathered by market research and Sales Executives of different zones. These are as below :

(i) The Market Research Department of the company has assessed that the product-Y is more popular in the market and if its price is increased by Rs. 4 per unit, it would not affect its sale volume adversely. The sale of product-z can be increased if its price is reduced by Rs. 4 per unit because it is over priced. Accordingly, the management takes decision to include these changes in its sales plan for 1998.

(ii) The Sales Executives of different zones have discussed the possible increase of the budgeted sales for the year, *i.e.* 1997 and product-wise estimation is made as given below :

(III)

Zones	*Estimated Increase in Sale (per cent)*		
	Product-X	*Product-Y*	*Product-Z*
North	15	30	10
South	05	15	15
East	12	25	12
West	15	20	10

(iii) The following possible sale increase is estimated in North and East Zones through trade exhibitions and intensive advertisement of the product :

(IV)

Zones	*Estimated Increase in Sale (Units)*		
	Product-X	*Product-Y*	*Product-Z*
North	4,000	3,200	2,400
East	10,400	5,000	3,200

Combined analysis of the above estimated changes for budgeted sales of next year over the budgeted sale of (1997) based on market research, sales executive assessment and by arranging effective exhibitions and intensive advertisement can be made as given on the next page.

(V)

Total Estimated Increase in Sales Volume and Price

Zones	Product-X		Product-Y		Product-Z	
	Change in Quantity	*Change in Price*	*Change in Quantity*	*Change in Price*	*Change in Quantity*	*Change in Price*
North	$\frac{40,000 \times 15}{100} = 6,000$	No Change	$\frac{32,000 \times 3}{100} = 9,600$	(+) 4	$\frac{60,000 \times 10}{100} = 6,000$	(–) 4
	(+) 4,000		(+) 3,200		(+) 2,400	
	10,000		12,800		8,400	
South	$\frac{48,000 \times 5}{100} = 2,400$	No Change	$\frac{28,000 \times 15}{100} = 4,200$	(+) 4	$\frac{40,000 \times 15}{100} = 6,000$	(–) 4
East	$\frac{20,000 \times 12}{100} = 2,400$	No Change	$\frac{36,000 \times 25}{100} = 9,000$	(+) 4	$\frac{60,000 \times 12}{100} = 7,200$	No Change
	(+) 10,400		(+) 5,000		(+) 3,200	
	12,800		14,000		10,400	
West	$\frac{80,000 \times 15}{100} = 12,000$	No Change	$\frac{40,000 \times 20}{100} = 8,000$	No Change	$\frac{48,000 \times 10}{100} = 4,800$	No Change

On the basis of the combined analysis made in table V and figures shown in table I, II, III, IV the comprehensive sales budget for the year 1998 can be prepared as shown in the next page :

Sales Budget for 1998

		Budgeted sale for 1997			*Actual Sale for 1997*			*Estimated increase in sale volume over the budgeted sale 1997*			*Budgeted sale for 1998*		
Zones	*Products*	*Units*	*Rate (Rs.)*	*Amount*	*Units*	*Rate (Rs.)*	*Amount*	*Units*	*Rate (Rs.)*	*Amount*	*Units*	*Rate (Rs.)*	*Amount*
NORTH	X	40,000	20	8,00,000	48,000	20	9,60,000	10,000	No Change	No Change	50,000	20	10,00,000
	Y	32,000	36	11,52,000	40,000	36	14,40,000	12,800	(–) 4	(–)51,200	44,800	40	17,92,000
	Z	60,000	64	38,40,000	52,000	64	33,28,000	8,400	(+)4	(+)33,600	68,400	60	41,04,000
SOUTH	X	48,000	20	9,60,000	40,000	20	8.00,000	2,400	No Change	No Change	50,400	20	10,08,000
	Y	28,000	36	10,08,000	32,000	36	11,52,000	4,200	(–)4	(–)16,800	32,200	40	12,88,000
	Z	36,000	64	23,04,000	36,000	64	23,04,000	6,000	(+)4	(+)24,000	42,000	60	25,20,000
EAST	X	20,000	20	4,00,000	32,000	20	6,40,000	12,800	No Change	No Change	32,800	20	6,56,000
	Y	36,000	36	12,96,000	28,000	36	10,08,000	14,000	(–)4	(–)56,000	50,000	40	20,00,000
	Z	60,000	64	38,40,000	56,000	64	35,84,000	10,400	(+)4	(+)41,600	70,400	60	42,24,000
WEST	X	80,000	20	16,00,000	88,000	20	17,60,000	12,000	No Change	No Change	92,000	20	18,40,000
	Y	40,000	36	14,40,000	32,000	36	11,52,000	8,000	(–)4	(–)32,000	48,000	40	19,20,000
	Z	48,000	64	30,72,000	60,000	64	38,40,000	4,800	(+)4	(+)19,200	52,800	60	31,68,000

Selling and Distribution Cost Budget

The selling and Distribution Cost Budget is prepared separately in the light of the budgeted sales volume of the enterprise. In adopting the comprehensive sales plan, the various expenses are incurred on account of selling and distribution. Selling covers all costs and responsibilities which affect demand for the products dealing with consumer and distribution. It includes the cost of packing, transporting and delivery. The amount spent on account of all these is included in the selling and distribution budget. While preparing this budget, the factors which are taken into consideration are :

(i) The ways and media through which the sale volume is channelised or affected.

(ii) The plans to be prepared for sales promotion.

(iii) The area and territories to be covered for sales.

(iv) Mode of distribution of the products.

With the consideration of the above factors, the budgetary provisions for selling and distribution expenses are made essentially for an integrated planning. "If budgetary control is to be integrated and co-ordinated fully, the selling and distribution cannot be ignored."[7] There should be a positive relationship between the selling and distribution expenses and volume to be sold in the market. Very often a business has to base the budget of selling and distribution costs on what it can afford in accordance with the objectives of the enterprise. Further, the reasonable level of selling expenses should be decided by the value being received from the sales efforts. The selling and distribution budget includes mainly two types of expenditures :

(i) Expenses incurred on account of the promotion of sales or selling cost.

(ii) Distribution expenses.

7. J. Batty, *Corporate Planning and Budgetary Control*, Macdonald and Evans Ltd., London, 1970. p. 254.

Selling cost

The expenditures relating to sale-promotion can be identified according to their nature, *i.e.*, fixed and variable. The expenses incurred on the salary of sales personnel, commission, travelling expenses, postage and stationery and any other perks paid to salesmen are variable ones. The salary paid to the administrative staff of Sales & Marketing Department, rent paid for sales offices and showrooms, administrative costs of sales office, depreciation on equipment and expenses incurred on advertising are included in the fixed expenditure. Advertisement is the main factor which affects sales in a positive direction and the expenses incurred on this account is the major constituent of selling and distribution budget. It is, therefore, essential to co-ordinate the advertising cost with the sales budget. The advertising cost should be based on the position of the company as well as on the income to be generated from it. In this regard, it is essential to measure the effectiveness of advertisements in the positive direction. This can be attempted by using any one of the following methods :

(a) **Selective Advertising.** This can be used in selective areas or specific fields which are typical of the market as a whole and its result in the market concerned is observed. If the result is positive, it is applied to the market as a whole by adjusting these results in the light of weighting factors for different conditions.

(b) **Simulation and Mathematical Technique.** The mathematical formula is employed relating to the past experience and future probabilities to show the likely results.

As a matter of fact, it is very difficult to assess the effectiveness of advertisement to a particular extent. It is because of the influence of many other factors like consumer's income, market competition, substitution effect in regard to affecting the sales in positive direction. Therefore, it is not always possible to establish the advertisement cost budget by relating the expenditure on advertisement to the extra income earned as a result of this.

The following factors should be taken into consideration while an advertisement cost budget is developed :

(i) Selection of the best method of the advertisements that can give maximum positive results.

(ii) The amount to be collected for the advertisement subject to the sales, profit, availability of fund and market competition.

Distribution Cost. Besides selling cost, the distribution of the product is another important factor that has to be taken into account for the preparation of a comprehensive sales plan. The expenses incurred from the dispatch of goods to its point of reach are included in distribution expenses. It is essential to make budgetary provisions properly for all such expenses. The steps, that may involve in the making of distribution cost budgets are :

(i) To select the mode of despatch of goods or proper transportation media;

(ii) Storage and warehouse facilities by products and area.

The marketing executives must be careful of safe and timely delivery of goods. It depends upon the nature and size of the product as well as the area that it covers. There may be variable and fixed distribution expenses. Expenses incurred on this account should also be based on the volume of sale and its return. Finally the expenses, that constitute selling cost, sales promotional cost and distribution cost, are altogether incorporated and accomplished. And then a budget for selling and distribution is prepared in the light of the objectives of the enterprise alongwith the sales budget. For this the proforma given on the next page can be used.

Format of Selling and Distribution Cost Budget

Functional Costs	*Fixed Element*	*Variable Element*	*Product-X*		*Product-Y*		*Product-Z*		*Total Sales*	
			Quantity	*Value*	*Quantity*	*Value*	*Quantity*	*Value*	*Quantity*	*Value*
1	2	3	4	5	6	7	8	9	10	11
(A) Selling Cost :										
(i) Variable Cost :										
(a) Salesman's Salary;										
(b) Salesman's Commission;										
(c) Travelling & Conveyance;										
(d) Postage & Stationery;										
(e) Telephone, etc.										
(ii) Fixed Cost :										
(a) Salary of Administrative Staff (sales);										
(b) Rent of Sales Office & show rooms;										
(c) Depreciation on equipments;										
(d) Insurance Premium of Sales Office.										
(B) Distribution Cost :										
(i) Transportation Costs;										
(ii) Storages and Warehousing Costs.										
(C) Advertising Cost :										
TOTAL:										

Production Budget

"The production budget is an estimate of the quantity of goods to be manufactured during the budget period."[8] After the developing of a comprehensive sales plan, it is essential to translate it into production budget as a basis for budgeting the various aspects of the operational functions. To prepare the production budget, the rates, forecast for each product, are combined alongwith the information about the beginning level and the expected level of ending inventories of the finished products.

The production budget can be developed with the following steps. At first production policies relating to inventory level should be established. Thereafter the total quantity of each product, that is to be manufactured, is estimated and at last it is scheduled according to interim periods. Thus, the quantities specified in the sales budget, adjusted to conform to production and inventory policies, give the volume of goods to be manufactured by product and by interim time period.

Production budget represents the Production Required = Sales Volume (±) Inventory Changes.

The preparation of production budget can be divided in to two parts, *i.e.*, (1) Production Volume Budget and (2) Production Cost Budget.

The Production Volume Budget is prepared in a quantitative form which includes the budgeted units to be manufactured during the budget period while the production cost budget is concerned only with the cost volume of budgeted units in relation to material, labour and overhead expenditures. The estimate of realistic production volume is necessary for the budgeting of material, labour and factory overhead expenses. Thus, the plan for production volume is the base for production cost budget.

The maximum production at a minimum (lowest) cost is possible only if it is determined with respect to optimum balance between sales, inventory and production levels. The production budget should not be over-emphasized because if it is so, the

8. Welsch, Glenn., *op. cit.*, 1976, p. 184.

other variables like cost, capital number of workers, etc. will automatically be affected.

For the development of production volume budget, important considerations for the following should be made :

(1) Production Requirements. The most important factor, that is to be taken into consideration while developing a production plan for a budget period, is to ascertain the requirements of total number of units to be manufactured during a budget period. It can be obtained by adjusting the sales budget as per the inventory changes. In this regard, the careful consideration of a number of subsidiary matters is essential. This should be assessed with the harmony of sales budget. Neither it should be over-estimated nor be under estimated. Overestimation will affect the other functional aspects relating to cost like raw material, labour, inventory position, capital, etc. Therefore, production executives should be very cautious in this context.

(2) Production Planning. Proper Production Planning is required to develop a production plan at an optimum level. For this the planners must determine an optimum balance between sales, inventory and production level. This they have to do very carefully because if the optimum balance is not achieved, many other aspects of the profit plan (budgeting) will be affected adversely. Therefore, a well balanced production programme is essential.

(3) Consideration of New Products. The idea for introducing a new product and changing old products raised by the Sales Executives should be seriously considered and finalised at the top level of management. In this regard, any decision should be taken in the light of objectives of the enterprise as a whole. As it may require some additional infrastructure at the time of initiation, the relating factors should be considered with respect to the time dimension.

(4) Production Capacity. It is necessary to ascertain the total production capacity of the plant in terms of both numbers and types of products. Subsequently, the optimum utilisation capacity of the plant should also be determined. Without taking these into consideration, the production planners cannot be able to achieve satisfactory results. The production capacity can be determined effectively with the harmony of plant utilisation budget. In this regard, it is important that the relating responsibility centre should not have an over optimistic approach. Adequacy of manufacturing facilities, *e.g.*, expansion or contraction of plant capacity should also be taken into consideration for the determination of plant capacity in relation to production plans.

(5) Inventory Policies. The level of stock, that is to be maintained, should be determined at the optimum level to minimise the production cost. Inventory is the determining factor for the production budget. The production volume is ascertained and budgeted by adding the closing inventory level of finished goods to the required units of sales for budget period and substracting the opening inventory balance. The possible amount of change relating to closing or opening balance of inventory should also be taken into consideration while preparing a production budget because such occurances will require additional production. Therefore, there must be a close co-ordination between production plan and inventory policies.

(6) Availability of Raw Materials, Purchase Components and Labour the production budget can give satisfactory results with respect to comprehensive profit planning and control only when it is based on a realistic approach. The availability of raw materials, labour or other purchase components are the fundamental issues on which any production plan is based. Without taking these into consideration, any plan made for production would prove to be only a blank sheet. It is, therefore, essential to make an accurate calculation about their stable sources with respect to time and costs. In this regard, the bye-products that are to be used in a final product should also be taken into consideration.

(7) Time Dimension. The time element is an important factor that cannot be ignored in developing a production plan. The time dimension should be identified with respect to both long run production plan and short-run production plan. Broad estimates of production levels necessary to project plant capacity requirements, factory costing structures, manpower requirements, cash flow and major anticipated change in inventory level, should be taken into considerations in developing a long-range plan. However, short-run production plan should be in harmony with the time dimension utilised in short-run profit plans. Very often it is developed for a period of one year divided into months and quarters.

(8) Goal of the Enterprise. It is the ultimate responsibility of top level management to evaluate and finalise the production plan in accordance with the objectives of the enterprise. Although a tentative production plan is developed by the executives of production department as they have first hand knowledge of plant and personnel capacity, availability of materials and the production situation, the policy decisions must be taken by the top management in this regard after taking into consideration various aspects affecting its goal.

At last, the approach used by a particular company depends upon the size and characteristics of its manufacturing process. A production budget can be developed with the help of the information given below :

The budgeted sale for an imaginary company as planned in sales budget for the various products, *e.g.*, X, Y and Z in different zones is given below.

PRODUCTS	*PLANNED SALES FOR DIFFERENT ZONES (UNITS)*				
	North Zone	*South Zone*	*East Zone*	*West Zone*	*Total*
X	50,000	50,400	32,800	92,000	2,25,200
Y	44,800	32,200	50,000	48,000	1,75,000
Z	68,400	42,000	70,400	52,800	2,33,600

However, some additional information regarding opening and closing inventory level for the year is also given below :

Inventory level of A. B. C. & Co. Ltd.

Products	*Closing Inventory of finished goods*	*Opening Inventory of finished goods*
X	1,25,300	1,45,000
Y	2,05,000	2,15,500
Z	1,67,000	1,78,400

From the above information, a production budget for the budget year 1998 can be prepared in the following form :

Production Budget of A. B. C. & Co. Ltd. for 1998

Products	*Units required for sale as per the sales budget*	*Add Closing inventory of finished goods*	*Total No. of units required*	*Less Opening inventory of finished goods*	*Units to be produced in budget year*
Product-X	2,25,200	1,25,300	3,50,500	1,45,000	2,05,500
Product-Y	1,75,000	2,05,000	3,80,000	2,15,500	1,64,500
Product-Z	2,33,600	1,67,000	4,00,600	1,78,400	2,22,200

Further, this annual plan may be brokenup into interim periods, *e.g.*, months and quarters for its effective implementation.

Note : Change in inventory level may be incorporated in the budget.

Production (Manufacturing) Cost Budget

After developing a plan for production volume, it is necessary to estimate the cost of production of units to be manufactured for which a budget for production cost is prepared. This budget constitutes mainly three cost components, *e.g.*, (i) Material Cost Budget, (ii) Direct Labour Cost Budget, and (iii) Factory Overheads Budget.

(1) Material Cost Budget. As per the production budget the required amount of raw material for each product is estimated. The material budget specifies these planned quantities of each raw material by time, by products and by using responsibility. In a manufacturing process, two types of materials are used. The first one is directly related to the production process and the second one is used in the maintenance of the manufacturing machines, *e.g.*, oil and lubricants, grease, etc. "The expenses incurred on direct material are included in Material Budget, while the expenses incurred on consumable raw materials are included (incorporated) in Factory Overheads Budget. The Material Budget deals only with quantities of direct materials."[9]

9. Welsch, Glenn., *op. cit.*, p. 213.

The following factors should be taken into consideration while developing the Material Cost Budget :

(i) *Raw Material Requirements* : On the basis of Production budget, the number of units to be manufactured are specified. Accordingly, the raw materials required for the production of these units are estimated. The required raw materials are classified with respect to quantity, cost and time. Inventory levels of raw materials should also be taken into consideration.

(ii) *Stocks of Raw Materials* : The maintenance of an optimum level of stock of the raw material is essential for the smooth running of the production process. "The level of stock of raw materials should be determined and maintained in such a way that cannot only assure the uninterrupted production process but also to keep the amount of stock capital locked in stocks as low as possible."[10]

The proper planning of the raw material prevents the accumulation of excess inventories which is essential to minimise the cost of production.

(i) The percentage of raw material to total cost of production should be calculated.

(ii) The cost of raw material required for the budgeted output should be reviewed in the light of current price trends with respect to different product groups and departments.

(iii) A summary of the amount of each kind of raw material required for each product group should be drawn-up.

(iv) The budgeted figures for raw material are classified in accordance with the product groups and departments. Simultaneously, the combined requirements of each product group for each type of raw material is summarised.

(v) Ratio of wastage and spoilage of material in the stock of store should be obtained from past records.

10. J.A. Scott., *Budgetary Control and Standard Cost*, Pitman Publishing, London, 1970, p. 36.

(vi) The tentative planned amount of raw material should be evaluated, synchronised and amended in accordance with the recommendations of the Purchase Department with respect to market price trends and sources of raw materials.

(vii) The time dimension between order and delivery of raw material must be taken into consideration for a suitable material budget.

After the requirement of raw material is ascertained, its availability should be ensured. In this regard, the preparation of a detailed schedule for the purchase of required raw material is needed. This is also known as Purchase Budget. "The Purchase Department is introduced with the raw materials requirement for the budget period by the Production Executives and Purchase Department proceed to find the most profitable means for meeting these requirements."[11]

The purchase budget specifies :

(i) the quantities of each type of raw material to be purchased;

(ii) the timing of the purchases and

(iii) the estimated cost of raw material to be purchased by unit as well as by the total.

In this regard the most important factor is to ensure the delivery of purchases within the stipulated time period so that the standard inventory level of raw material can be maintained. The value of opening stocks must, therefore, be considered and the value to which it is desired to increase or decrease stocks at the end of the budget period must be taken into account before budgeting for the materials to be purchased. In order to make it sure that a certain part of goods arrives on specified dates as and when required as per the production programme, a detailed schedule should be made up by both the Planning and Purchase Departments.

---

11. J.A. Scott., *Budgetary Control and Standard Cost*, Pitman Publishing, London, 1970, p. 39.

The material requirements for the replacement of scrap should not be forgotten. The determination of the rate of consumption is very essential for an effective material budgeting. This can be ascertained only with the close co-ordination between Planning, Purchase and Stores Departments.

The purchase budget should be developed with respect to both long run and short run. In this regard, the most vital factor is the policy of management because the purchase of raw materials directly affects the fund position of the company. Availability of funds and storage facilities should also be taken into account by the Purchase Executives while making an effective purchase plan.

A definite purchase plan makes possible a better organisation and at the same time brings about more efficiency in Purchasing Department operation with a consequent cost reduction and improved cash-flow.

(ii) Direct Labour Budget or Labour Cost Budget

The estimate of direct labour requirements necessary to produce the types and quantities of output planned in the production budget is called direct labour budget. Labour is the second important factor which is considered for drawing up a production budget. Since the labour cost is the main element among the different constituents of costs of production, it is essential to make a careful planning and systematic control of labour costs.

Labour is generally classified as direct labour and indirect labour. The wages and incentives paid to the employees directly engaged in a specific production function are included in the direct labour budget. The costs of indirect labour such as, supervisory staff's salary and wages paid to tool makers, storekeepers and repairing staff are incorporated in the factory overheads budget.

The direct labour budget should be developed in terms of responsibility direct labour and direct labour costs, by product and interim periods as well as by responsibility centres.

(i) The first step in developing a labour budget is to estimate the total number of labour personnel required for production in each department. This requirement is classified under the headings of different classes of labour as per grades and trades.

(ii) The standard time (labour hours) is determined for each unit of each product. It can be done through any one of various approaches like time and motion studies, standard cost accounting system, statistical estimates or direct estimates by supervisors, etc.

(iii) The next step is to find out the average wage rate for direct labour for each department or cost centre. This is done with the help of the standard costing section. But where the standard costing system is not being adopted, the past figures or historical data may be used as the base of calculating average wage rates.

(iv) Thereafter this budget is converted into monetary terms by multiplying the standard time with the average wage rate for each unit of product. And thus, the per unit labour cost of product as well as the total direct labour cost for each product is found out.

The figures of total manpower requirement and its cost are analysed, revised and adjusted in the light of the proposed expansion, technical consideration and price fluctuations. For any capital extension, the long-run direct labour and personnel budget is prepared.

The introduction of a new scheme regarding incentives, overtime, etc. should also be taken into consideration while estimating the direct ratio of labour cost to some measure of output that can be projected realistically.

(iii) Factory Overheads Budget

The third important element of Production Cost Budget is factory overheads (manufacturing expenses). it is, therefore essential to prepare a separate budget for manufacturing expenses. This includes mainly a separate budget for manufacturing expenses *e.g.*, expenses incurred on the salary of supervisory staff and wages of all other staff who are not directly related to the production process such as, repairs, maintenance, storage, etc. This is also known as indirect labour cost. The expenses incurred on consumable raw materials such as oil, lubricants, electricity, etc., that are essential for the maintenance of machines relating to production department are known as indirect material costs. It also includes the insurance costs. This budget should be developed for the responsibility centres of Production and Services Departments. The overheads budget should be developed in the light of interim time periods. It is developed simultaneously with the direct material and direct labour budgets so that with the consolidation of these budgets, a comprehensive budget for production cost can be drawnup.

While developing the manufacturing expenses budget the following points must be considered carefully :

(a) The plan for indirect labour should be made in such a way as its cost may bear some normal ratio to direct labour cost. The budgeted figure for this item can usually be drafted in the light of past experience. It should be estimated at the various volumes of production differently and then collective cost should be justified with the total quantity of output. The figures of indirect labour and expenses incurred on these should be obtained with the consultation of Foreman and Works Superintendent and expressed clearly with respect to the related output.

(b) The indirect materials like oil and grease, waste, types of small tools, etc. to be used in manufacturing process should also be budgeted properly. It should be forecast in the light of various volumes of production based on a previous experience. In this regard it is important that the elimination of wastage should be watched constantly. For this, a haphazard purchasing of such items should be avoided and a standard level of inventory be maintained.

(c) The expenses, incurred in a department serving other departments and not directly concerned with the production, should be allocated rationally. These are mainly the expenses incurred on heating, lighting, power, maintenance, inspection, internal transport, storage, receiving and despatch and tool rooms, etc. Since the costs, incurred on these, constitutes a meaningful ratio to the total cost, it is suggested that the management should be much cautious of them.

(d) Repairs and maintenance should be a part of regular routine of inspection, testing and overhauling and it should never be carried out in a haphazard fashion. In spite of the careful efforts made in this respect, there may be exceptional breakdowns. It is therefore, essential that a suspense account to an optimum proportion as to the actual cost should be charged consistently so that the cost fluctuation may be minimised. All repairs and overhauls should be anticipated and budgeted to a possible extent and should be spread over for the total budget period evenly.

(e) A possible destination should be made in between the fixed and variable expenses. The expenses that tend to persist at a fixed level for no means of output *e.g.*, rent, rates, insurance and depreciation, etc. should be allocated under the fixed expenses. The expenses, which tend to vary with the changes in volume of output like power, consumable items, etc., should be treated as variable expenses.

Keeping in view the expenses incurred on account of the above mentioned variables, a comprehensive budget for the factory overheads may be prepared in both the physical as well as monetary terms.

"The expenditure is initially compiled in terms of quantities, *e.g.*, physical units for materials, labour hours for wages, etc. and then converted into rupee value by applying the budgeted price of material and the budgeted rates of wages. The total of these estimated expenses separately for fixed and variable and for each department constitutes the expenses budget for the department."[12]

The tentative plan for manufacturing expenses should be chalked out by the costing section with the consultation of the departmental heads of production units (shops). Thereafter the budgeted works overhead should be analysed by the budget section and be adjusted in the light of the production cost budget.

With the compilation of material budget, direct labour budget and factory overheads budget, a comprehensive budget for production cost may be presented in the following formats :

12. Prasad, N.K., *op. cit.*, pp. 16-21.

A Comprehensive Budget for Production Cost

		Material			*Labour*					*Factory Overhead*				
Products	*Department Items*	*Quantity Required*	*Rate*	*Cost per Unit (Rs.)*	*Operation*	*Trade & Grade*	*Wage per Hour*	*Rate per Hour*	*Cost per Unit (Rs.)*	*Dep-artm--ent*	*Fixed*	*Variable*	*Cost per Unit (Rs.)*	*Total Cost of Product-ion*
PRODUCT-X														
PRODUCT-Y														
PRODUCT-Z														
TOTAL														

Administrative Expenses Budget

The administrative expenses include operational costs other than manufacturing and distribution expenses. Two types of expenses are mainly included in this. First one is the expenses incurred in regard to the payment of salary to the office staff and other administrative and managerial personnel. Secondly, it includes all the expenses incurred on account of maintenance and running of administrative sections like office stationery, electricity, insurance, etc.

The proper budgeting for administrative expenses is essential because "there is a strong tendency not to pinpoint responsibility for costs of a general nature or those incurred in large part by top management."[13] The magnitude and effect of such expenses on profit potential is generally overlooked due to which difficulty arises in developing a proper plan for such expenditures.

"There should be little difficulty in budgeting the figures for administration which will cover the expenses of all the central offices and management salaries. The real difficulty lies in the subsequent fair allocation of the cost."[14] Excepting a few variable expenses, a large portion of administrative expenses is fixed and uncontrollable. Therefore, most of the enterprises make a provision for such expenses in factory overheads budget because of its being more convenient to them.

Administrative expenses budget should be developed by the managers of each responsibility centre for their own department separately at the grassroot level. Thereafter a combined budget for all the departments should be prepared by the budget section. The historical data can be used as a base to forecast these expenses in a best way because they do not fluctuate much.

This budget should also be co-ordinated with other functional budgets for an effective profit planning and control. A certain standard should be fixed with respect to total sales volume so

---

13. Welsch, Glenn, *op. cit.*, p. 276.

14. J.A., Scott., *Budgetary Control and Standard Costs*, Pitman Publishing, London, 1970, p. 47.

that these expenses may be kept within limit. "Since the administrative function is primarily concerned with providing a service, the manager has to ensure that this is done at a reasonable Cost."[15] The range of administrative functioning is very vast. Therefore, the top management has to co-ordinate all activities and ensure their economical operation.

The entire amount of administrative expenses is to be forecast for the budget year. Thereafter, it is to be divided by months and quarters so as to make a fair allocation of budgeted amount.

This budget can be developed in the format given below :

Administrative Expenses Budget

Department	*Inputs*	*Annual*	*First Quarter*			*Second Quarter*	*Third Quarter*	*Fourth Quarter*
			Jan.	*Feb.*	*March*			
(A) Administrative Department								
(a) Supervisory Salaries								
(b) Travelling & Entertainment								
(c) Telephone & Telegraph								
(d) Depreciation								
(e) Insurance								
(f) Taxes								
(g) Stationery & Office Supplies								
(h) Audit Fee								
TOTAL								
(B) Accounting Department								
(C) Cash Department								
Total of all Departments :								
Allocated Building Service Cost :								
TOTAL COST								

15. J. Batty, *Corporate Planning and Control*, Macdonald and Evens Ltd., London, 1970, p. 158.

Plant Utilisation Budget

Plant Utilisation Budget is a quantitative budget just like production budget. Machines used in the production process are not less important than material or man and are directly related to the production volume. Therefore, it is essential to make a detailed programme regarding the number and working hours of these by department, by product and by times co-ordinating with the sales and production plans. The sales budget, the production budget and the plant utilisation budget must be perfectly linked with one another so that there will neither be a shortfall in meeting the sales requirements nor overstocking of finished goods in the factory or an uneconomic utilisation of the available plant facilities. A proper co-ordination among these budgets is must so that any problem regarding over-stocking or shortage may be uprooted at the proper time.

The plant utilisation budget should be forecast in such a way so as to meet the sudden additional sales requirement. This can be met by working overtime, by transferring the work to the departments having surplus capacity or passing it to petty contractors. To elevate the plant economy, the existing plant facilities should be utilised to the maximum level of their capacity.

The following factors should be taken into consideration for the development of Plant Utilisation Budget :

(1) Requirement of Machine. The department-wise requirement of machine should be obtained by the Plant Managers. The sales and production budget can be a base for finding out such requirements.

(2) Working Hours. The planning for the utilisation of machines should be made in the light of sales-requirement. The. working hours should be fixed with the harmony of standard capacity of the plant and machinery.

(3) Depreciation. Replacement of machines is a major cost bearing factor in the production process. Therefore, depreciation should be charged with a reasonable ratio to the total cost of machine. The price variation should also be taken into consideration for this purpose.

(4) New Inventions. The plant budget planners should be attentive to new inventions in context to the plant and machineries to enable them to face world-wide competitions. It is essential to adopt newer techniques to minimise the cost of production.

(5) Normal Working Loss. The hourly loss of working should also be estimated for each machine. The past figures can be a base to forecast it. Further, the hourly operating expenses of the plant and machinery should also be forecast.

(6) Cash Requirements. Any addition of new machine or newer technique requires a huge involvement of cash. The budget for a plant should be prepared in accordance with total amount of cash to be involved, time and period and expected returns.

By incorporating the above factors, a tentative plant utilisation budget is prepared by the managers of different cost centres. Then it is compiled by the Budget Section into an integrated form and is submitted to the management for its approval. Thereafter, it is evaluated and adjusted by the top management in the light of the policies of the company and general economic and market conditions.

This budget can be developed in the format given at next page :

Plant Utilisation Budget for the Budget Year

PRODUCT	*TIME PERIOD*	*UNITS TO BE PRODUCED*	*COST CENTRE-A*			*COST CENTRE -B*			*COST CENTRE-C*		
			Required Hours per Unit	*Total Machine Hours Reqd.*	*No.of Machines Reqd.*	*Required Hours per Unit*	*Total Machine Hours Reqd.*	*No. of Machines Reqd.*	*Required Hours per Unit*	*Total Machine Hours Reqd.*	*No. of Machines Reqd.*
PRODUCT- X	1st Quarter:										
	January										
	February										
	March										
	TOTAL:										
	2nd Quarter :										
	April										
	May										
	June										
	TOTAL :										
	3rd Quarter:										
	July										
	August										
	September										
	TOTAL:										
	4th Quarter:										
	October										
	November										
	December										
	TOTAL										
PRODUCT-Y											
PRODUCT-Z											
	GRAND TOTAL										

Research and development Budget

The expenses incurred on research and development programme are included in this budget. Today a huge amount is spent on this account by most of the business organisations. Due to a worldwide competition and rapid change in the field of business and industry, it has become essential to adopt continuing research programmes to face these challenges successfully. The main objectives of research and development programmes are :

(a) To acquire better basic knowledge and know how.

(b) To create new products, process, services and equipment so as to improve the company's financial position by maximising profit.

(c) to improve upon the existing products, process, etc. This should be with a view to retaining or enlarging profits by keeping the products competitive in quality and price and by making them more acceptable to the market.

(d) To find new uses of products process, etc.

(e) To explore the possibilities of obtaining and retaining a large market.

(f) To find better methods of service to customers.

(g) To search for opportunities of expansion into other fields which may or may not be related to the present business. The intention, of course, is to increase profits through such diversification.

Thus, the expenses, incurred on this account, cannot be linked directly to the production result as in case of other operational budgets. Therefore, the basis of budgetary provisions of such expenses can also be different.

Since it includes the variety of objects, expenditure incurred on this account can have different accounting treatments in different circumstances.

To fulfil these objectives basic research and applied research is carried out in a business concern. As the research and development includes the important aspects of the process, the expenses incurred on this account can be put under two separate heads, *i.e.*, research cost and development cost. Research cost is defined as the cost of searching for new or improved products, new applications of materials or new improved methods. It includes the cost of initial experiments, tests and subsequent small-scale trial runs to prove the results of the research. The expenditure is normally comprised of wages and salaries of the research and testing staff materials and facilities utilised in laboratory and research department, payment to outside research organisation. The other important aspect is the development aspect. The development cost is the cost of process which begins with the implementation of the decision to produce a new or improved product or to employ a new or improved method and ends with the commencement.

The research and development cost incurred with respect to searching of new products is of the nature of pre-production cost which is incurred much before the actual production is started. At the time of expenditure either there is no production or there is very small production. Therefore, only reasonable portion of such expenditures should be charged for the on-going production and rest should be deferred for future period till the full-fledged production is started. Further, it should be distributed over the number of years as benefited by the research and development programmes.

The expenses incurred on the research and development activities carried out with a view to improving the existing product should be charged as a part of the current expenditure. As these are incurred to improve the general working of the enterprise in all the functionaries *e.g.*, works, office, marketing, etc., the spent amount should be distributed properly among the factory overheads and selling and distribution overheads.

The proper budgeting is essential to have an effective control over the research and development expenditures and tends to coordinate itself with the other plans. The long-run and short-run budgets should be developed with a view to geting the maximum possible advantages of the future market conditions as well as a fair return on investment. The planning regarding research expenses is difficult because research activities cannot be tied to a strict time schedule while the planning regarding developmental activities is easier as it can be tied to the time schedule.

The following important steps are involved in the development of research and development budget :

(1) Determination of Objectives. The objectives of Research and Development Work, that is to be carried out, should be clearly defined at first. This can be done in terms of introduction of a new product, new technique, improvement in facilities and consumer service and cost reduction, etc.

(2) Determination of Responsibility. Before undertaking the work, centre of responsibility must be determined. Then it should be assigned to the department concerned with a particular objective.

(3) Determination of Plan Period. The third important step is to establish long-run and short-run budgets for Research and Development Programme. The long-run. planning is made to ensure that the organisation is able to get the maximum possible advantage of the future market conditions. The short-run planning for such expenditures is made with a view to seeing that only those research and development works are undertaken which give a fair return on the investment.

(4) Determination of Expenditure Limit. The limit of the expenditures incorporated in both the long-run and short-run budgets should be fixed by department, project or centre. For this, the fund position and availability of fund must be taken into consideration because any shortage of fund can affect the programme adversely. The historical data can be a base for fixing the limit for future programmes. It can be determined to a certain percentage of total sales volume or total profit.

(5) Determination of Priority. Since the Research and Development Programmes cover a very vast range of activities, it is essential to fix priorities before the work is undertaken. These priorities are ascertained by the Project Managers in the form of a research project.

(6) Performance Evaluation and Re-appraisal. Since a research project is completed in a number of years, the performance evaluation and its reappraisal is essential from time to time. The performance evaluation is required to assess the expenditures incurred in accordance with the budgetary provisions and limits consistently. However, during the course of research work, the market conditions may change, like-wise the need for a modification or discontinuance of project may arise. Therefore, a re-appraisal of the project is necessary.

Cash Budget

The adoption of production budget or sales budget cannot be approved until and unless the arrangement for the required working capital is made. Therefore, it is essential to develop a realistic cash plan before finalising the other functional budgets. "A cash budget is a summary statement of the firm's expected cash inflows and outflows over a projected time period."[16] Thus, the cash budget presents the total inflows and outflows of cash during the budget period. Cash budgeting involves a projection of cash inflows, outflows and financing need coupled with a cash control. It gives information on the timing and magnitude of expected cash flows and cash balances over the projected period. This information helps the financial managers to paln the future cash needs of the firm and exercise control over its cash and liquidity. The cash budget helps to maintain an optimum cash balance. If a deficit in cash is expected, the additional arrangements are made immediately to meet it. On the other hand, if there is a surplus cash position, this amount can be put to more profitable uses.

Though the cash budget provides a foundation for other functional budgets, cash is realised mainly through sales. Therefore, a close co-ordination is needed between sales budget and cash budget. The main objectives of cash budget may be outlined as follows :

1. To estimate the expected cash position as a result of planned operations.
2. To indicate the need for borrowing of ideal cash for investment.

16. Pandey, I.M., *Financial Management*, 1979, Vikash Publication House, New Delhi, p. 304.

3. To indicate the deficit or surplus position of cash.
4. To make cash compatible with total working capital, sales, investment and debt.
5. To provide a sound basis for credit.
6. To establish a sound basis for an effective control over cash.

The cash budget is prepared by the Chief Finance Manager with the co-ordination of all other departmental heads. This is prepared in two parts :

(i) Cash inflows or receipt of cash.

(ii) Cash outflows or disbursement of cash.

(i) *Receipt of Cash* : In this part of the budget, the total amount of cash inflows is forecast for the entire budget period. Thereafter, it is broken into month-wise actual receipt of cash. The main sources of cash receipts are : (i) Cash sales, (ii) Realisation from debtors and bills receivables, (iii) Dividend (iv) Royalty, (v) Rent, Interest and Commission, (vi) Issue of shares and debentures, (vii) Sale of assets and properties and (viii) Borrowings.

(ii) *Disbursement of Cash* : The total expected expenditure to be incurred during the budget period is included in this part of the budget. The planned expenditure figures are obtained from all departments, *i.e.*, purchase, labour, works, administration, etc. with the compilation of these figures, the total outflow of cash is estimated. This part of the budget includes mainly the cost of direct material and direct labour, selling and distribution expenses, administrative expenses, payment of royalty, rent, interest, commission, dividend and government taxes, etc. It also includes the repayment of loans. The total expected amount of outflows is also spread over month-wise required disbursement. The cash budget can be prepared with the following methods :

(i) Receipt and Payment Method;

(ii) Profit Adjustment Method and

(iii) Balance Sheet Method.

(i) *Receipt and Payment Method* : This method is used mainly for a short-term cash budgeting. For the long-run cash budgeting, this method is not appropriate. By using this method the total receipt and disbursement of cash for the budget period is estimated. The cash inflows are planned by incorporating all functional budgets and sources of funds, thereby adding to the opening balance of cash. Simultaneously, the total amount to be disbursed in a budget period is also estimated. The total amount of disbursement is subtracted from the amount of total cash receipts. Thus, the closing balance of cash is found out.

The following information regarding cash inflows and outflows of X, Y & Z Co. Ltd., are given for a period of six months ending on 30th June, 1998.

Months	*Sales (Rs.)*	*Material consumed (Rs.)*	*Wages (Rs.)*	*Production Overheads (Rs.)*	*Office and Selling Overheads (Rs.)*
January	52,000	15,000	6,000	4,000	3,500
February	77,000	21,000	8,100	4,300	4,700
March	66,000	15,500	6,600	4,000	5,500
April	68,600	20,600	12,000	4,500	6,900
May	82,500	27,000	16,000	6,000	9,000
June	87,700	28,800	18,000	6,200	9,500

The following additional information are also given in this regard :

1. 50 per cent of total sales are cash sales.
2. An asset is to be acquired in the month of April for which provisions should be made for the payment of Rs. 20,000.
3. In the month of May, an amount of Rs. 25,000 borrowed from a bank.
4. Rs. 25,000 is to be paid on account of dividend in June.
5. Debtors are allowed one month's credit.
6. One month's credit is granted by the creditors for material purchased and overheads.

7. Commission at 5 per cent on sales is paid to the salesmen in each month.
8. Opening balance of cash on January 1, 1995 is Rs. 62,500.

On the basis of the above mentioned information the cash plan for the period can be prepared as under :

Cash Budget of the X. Y. Z Co. Ltd. for the first half year ending as on 30th June, 1998

Period	*January*	*February*	*March*	*April*	*May*	*June*	*Total*
Receipts of Cash :							
Cash Sales	26,000	38,500	33,000	34,300	41,250	43,850	2,16,900
Receipt from Debtors	—	26,000	38,500	33,000	34,300	41,250	1,73,050
Money borrowed from Bank	—	—	—	—	25,000	—	25,000
TOTAL	**26,000**	**64,500**	**71,500**	**67,300**	**1,00,550**	**85,100**	**4,14,950**
Payments :							
Material	—	15,000	21,000	15,500	20,600	27,000	99,100
Wages	6,000	8,100	6,600	12,000	16,000	18,000	66,700
Production Overheads	—	4,000	4,300	4,000	4,500	6,000	22,800
Office & Selling Expenses	—	3,500	4,700	5,500	6,900	9,000	29,600
Capital Expenditures	—	—	—	20,000	—	—	20,000
Dividend	—	—	—	—	—	25,000	25,000
Commission on Sales	2,600	3,850	3,300	3,430	4,125	4,385	21,690
TOTAL	**8,600**	**34,450**	**39,900**	**60,430**	**52,125**	**89,385**	**2,84,890**
Net Cash Flow	26,000	64,500	71,500	67,300	1,00,550	85,100	4,14,950
Opening Balance of the months	62,500	79,900	1,09,950	141,550	1,48,420	1,96,845	1,92,560
Closing Balance	**79,900**	**1,09,950**	**1,41,550**	**1,48,420**	**1,96,845**	**1,92,560**	**3,22,620**

(2) Profit Adjustment Method. This method is more appropriate for making a long run cash budget (Projections). Under this method the income statement (Profit and Loss Account) is converted into a cash budget. This method is based on the basic approach that the cash balance is directly associated with the profit results. Every amount of profit results is an increase in the cash balance. This method may be useful as a means of checking the accuracy of the final balance shown by the receipt and payment method of forecast. The expected net profit, assets and liabilities of the current period, capital receipts and expenditures and payment on dividends, are the important factors that should be taken into consideration while preparing the cash budget by this method.

By this method, the cash budget can be prepared in the format given below :

Cash Budget

Particulars	*Period*						
Quarter	*1st Quarter*	*2nd Quarter*	*3rd Quarter*	*4th of the*	*Total Year 1st Year*	*2nd Year*	*3rd*
1	2	3	4	5	6	7	8
Opening Balance of the Cash							
Add :							
Budgeted Net Profit							
Capital Receipts							
Issue of Shares and Debentures							
Accrued Expenses							
Reserves							
Depreciation							
Reduction in Stocks							
Reduction in Debtors							
TOTAL							
Subtract :							
Capital Expenditures							
Dividends							
Capital Refunds							
Decrease in Liability							
Increase in Stock							
Increase in Debtors							
TOTAL							
Closing Balance							

Balance Sheet Method

By this method, the cash position is estimated by preparing a tentative balance sheet for the budget period. The items of assets and liabilities are shown in the balance sheet. The difference amount of liabilities and assets is treated as cash balance. This method is useful only for a long-run cash budgeting. The estimate of cash position can be obtained by adding the amount of decrease in assets and increase in liabilities to opening cash balance and by subtracting the value of decrease in liabilities and increase in assets from this. Thus, closing balance of cash is forecast for the budget period.

After calculating the closing balance of cash by any of the above mentioned methods, the next step is to determine the financing needs. Cash inflows and outflows are compared to assess the planned cash position throughout the budget period. If there is a deficit in any month, it requires to make additional arrangements for financing to meet the deficit and if a surplus fund is available, a provision should be made to invest it in a profitable manner :

Master Budget

The budget, that is finally approved, adopted and employed in an organisation, is called the Master Budget. It incorporates the budget estimates relating to all important functionaries of the organisation. Based on it the budgeted P&L A/c and the Balance-sheet are prepared.

Budget Classification — on the basis of Capacity

On the basis of capacity, two types of budgets are prepared (i) Fixed Budget and (ii) Flexible Budget.

(i) *Fixed Budget* : The budget prepared for a particular level of output not modified or adjusted in accordance with the actual output is very often known as fixed budget. The fixed budgets are more useful for a small period of time when there is not much possibility of variation between the actual performance and budgeted amount. The research and development budgets and advertising expenses budgets are the most suitable example of fixed budgets because to process these activities, a fixed amount is allocated to meet the budget centre's expenditures as they do not vary with the volume of production.

The effective cost control for the budget centres is not possible by the application of fixed budget. The real cause of variance of the actual expenses at actual level of production cannot be identified through it. Therefore, it can be used in a very limited sphere of the concern.

(ii) *Flexible Budget* : It is not easy to achieve the planned level of output for a business enterprise because of so many uncertainties prevailing in the field of business and industry. It is, therefore, essential to prepare a budget in such a way that can set the different levels of standards with respect to cost and output. This is known as flexible budgeting. "Flexible budgeting is a technique whereby budgets are complied to cover a number of possible outputs and their related costs."[17] Under this the budgeted revenue and costs are adjusted for the actual output achieved at different levels throughout the budget period.

The concept of cost variability is the underlying foundation of flexible budgeting. Variable budgets are schedules of costs or expenses indicating how each expense should change with changes in volume of output or activity. It explains as to what a specific expense should be at various levels.

The central objective of the variable budget approach is to identify more specifically the means and extent of each item of expenses that is influenced by the amount of work done in a responsibility centre. The expenses incurred on actual basis are compared with the allocated budgeted expenditures and a revised plan is made by adjusting variances.

Budget Classification — On the Basis of Conditions

(i) Basic Budget. This type of budget is prepared mainly for those activities which are not fully controllable. This is prepared as per the standard norms prevailing in the long-run. This cannot be used for the purpose of control. Therefore, it is effective only in forming policies and taking decisions by the top management.

---

17. J. Batty, *Corporate Planning and Budgetary Control*, (Macdonald and Evan Ltd., London), 1970, p. 276.

(ii) Current Budget. This budget is developed on the basis of analysing the current position of the market. This type of budget is prepared only for a short period because the market conditions change very sharply.

Budget Classification — On the basis of Periods

(i) Long-run Budget. A long-run budget is prepared normally for five to ten years and is further divided yearly. There are certain expenditures which are incurred much before the actual result is obtained and the benefits of certain expenditures are achieved over a number of years. These expenditures are called capital expenditures. The long-run budget is mainly prepared for such expenditures.

(ii) Short-run Budget. The short-run budget involves a period of one year or less than this. Operational and revenue budgets are prepared as short-run budgets. The period of budget is further broken into interim period, *e.g.*, half yearly, quarterly and monthly.

Today both the national and international conditions are changing rapidly. Therefore, the preparation of a realistic budget in accordance with the prevailing market conditions is essential for any business concern.

4

Budgeting — Capital Expenditures

The effective management of capital is the most important function of financial management today. The important aspect of budgetary control is to make a suitable plan for the investment of its fund in long-term assets and other profitable activities. These investment decisions are known as the capital budgeting. "The capital budgeting decision of a firm involves the decision to invest its fund most efficiently in long-term activities in anticipation of an expected flow of future benefits over a series of years."[1] It is essential to take such decisions because no firm can remain static today in the changing conditions of the business world. A continuous effort is required to make proper plans for expansion, construction, modernisation and development.

Long run objectives of a company usually provide for expansion of plants, distribution facilities, sources of raw materials and other resources which require capital expenditures financed by retained earnings by equity or by debt secured from outside. The capital budgeting is an important tool to manage the capital expenditures. "Capital budgeting involves the entire process of planning expenditures whose returns are expected to extend beyond one year."[2] The capital expenditures are incurred with a view to the profit over and above these expenses, so these expenses are treated as investment. "Most expenditures for plants, equipments and other long lived assets affect operations

1. Agrawal, J.D., *Capital Budgeting Decisions under Risk and Uncertainty*, 1988, Indian Institute of Finance, Delhi, p. 7
2. J. Fred Weston & Eugene F. Brighan, *Managerial Finance*, 1977, p. 283.

over a series of years. They are large, permanent commitments that influence long run flexibility and earning power."[3]

The capital budgeting decisions are the most crucial and critical decisions of the business. Any decision concerning the long run investment has a decisive influence on the rate and direction of the growth. It requires an assessment of future events which are most uncertain and can affect all aspects of an organisation. "Since all facets of a business are affected by capital expenditure-decisions, there is a need to consider the likely consequences of any acquisition not only on finance but also on future overall efficiency. Production, selling, administration and research and development are all likely to be affected by a single decision to purchase a major item of plant."[4] Therefore, any decision in this regard should not be considered in the isolation of a single cost centre, but an overall view with respect to consequences of such decisions should be taken into account for an effective use of resources. It is also necessary to define the objectives of a plan clearly..... "Definition of objectives and plans gives the key as to what basically to do, where to place the primary emphasis and what to accomplish by the network of policies, procedures, budgets and programmes."[5]

The capital budgeting decisions involve the commitment of a large amount of funds. "The need for substantial amount of funds for capital budgeting makes it imperative for the firm to plan its investment programmes very carefully and to make advance arrangement for procuring finance. Since fixed investment decisions are crucial to the health and survival of a business, they involve the commitment of huge sums for long periods and a single mistake can have a disastrous effect on the profitability and also survival of the firm."[6] The top management is constantly faced with the problems of determining the amount of funds to

3. Charles T. Horngrem, *Cost Accounting and Managerial Emphasis*, Prentice Hall of India Pvt. Ltd., New Delhi, 1976, p. 452.

4. J. Batty, *op. cit.*, p. 176.

5. Koontz, Herald and O. Donnel, Cyril, *Principle of Management*, (New York, MC Graw, Hill Book Company, Inc., p. 44.

6. Agrawal, G.D., *op. cit.*, p. 9.

be invested in fixed plants. Therefore, a special care should be taken to find out the solution of the problems. The basic problem revolves around necessity to maintain adequate facilities for growth and for meeting customers demand. On the other hand, considerable planning and control are necessary to prevent over-investment in operating capacity and investment in assets producing a low return on the funds committed.

Though the capital expenditures are incurred with a view to earning profit, there are certain projects from which it is difficult to measure the rate of return. "The accuracy of rate of return estimates varies widely among different types of investments and there are some types for which no estimates can be made at all...... certain over-riding strategic consideration should shelter some kinds of investments from the full rigours of rate of return rivalry and given them preference in capital budgeting."[7]

From the point of view of the involvement of funds, return and time dimension, the capital expenditures can be classified as under :

(i) Tactical and strategic decisions;

(ii) Profit earning projects and non-profit earning projects and

(iii) Short-run plans and long-run plans.

Tactical and Strategic Decisions

Tactical investment decisions involve relatively small amount of funds and do not result in a departure from the previous activities of the firm. This could be an investment proposal designated to reduce costs in the output of existing products without altering the scale of operation. This may be in the form of mechanisation of a process, replacing or modernising a process or choosing between alternative machines. On the other hand, strategic investment decisions involve large sums of money and may result in a major departure from the previous activities of the firm, *i.e.,* proposal to add new products to the product lines.

7. Dean, Joel, Capital Budgeting — *Top Management Policy on Plant Equipment & Product*, New York, Columbia University Press, 1962, p. 82.

Profit Earning Projects

Direct profit earning projects are the projects that provide a direct addition to net profit, *i.e.*, purchase of a new machine, replacement of assets which is expected to increase production. The indirect earning projects are the projects which may result from attempting to develop a new product or idea. It includes the research and development projects and educational and training projects.

Non-Profit Earning Projects

The capital expenditures incurred on account of welfare schemes and safety measures, etc. are put into this category. It includes mainly the expenses relating to the development of transport and sports facilities for the employees, provision for accident prevention devices and fire preventive devices. A provision for such expenditures is made to boost-up the moral of the employees which contributes to increase productivity indirectly.

Short-run Plans and Long-run Plans

As per the time dimension, the capital expenditure budget can be classified into short-run plans and long-run plans. The capital budgets are usually prepared for more than a year but the time dimension may differ as per the nature of the project. The projects, that require two to three years of time, are put under the short-run plans whereas the long-run plans involve more time, *i.e.,* 5 to 25 years.

Sizer has formally defined the long-range planning as a "systematic and formalised process for purposefully directing and controlling the future operation of a company towards desired objectives for period beyond one year. Long range planning should cover a period long enough to provide management with opportunity to anticipate future problems and thus to have sufficient freedom of action to resolve them in an ordinary manner."[8]

Once the project concerning the capital expenditure is

---

8. Sizer, John, *An Insight into the Management Accounting*, Richard Clay (The Chauser Press Ltd.), 1979, p. 235.

undertaken, it cannot be stopped suddenly because of its irreversible nature. Abandonment of such decisions results in a heavy financial loss. The twin characteristics of irreversibility and risk give rise to the critical importance of .capital budgeting in the management of the company. With the growing complexity and highly specific character of modern production and marketing methods, investment decisions are becoming more irreversible. Thus, "investment decisions are increasingly determining the direction and place of company's future growth and limit the opportunities open to it in much the same that the tracks determine the speed and direction open to a locomotive."[9]

The capital budgeting decisions provide the planning, co-ordination and control of the capital expenditures. Under the process of planning, they facilitate a sound planning for capital expenditures with respect to the future goals of an enterprise. Secondly, they make an effective co-ordination of capital related to financial needs, investment committed to the various functionaries, sales and profit potentials. Under the control function, they work as a check-valve in regard to major and minor capital expenditures.

Process of Capital Budgeting

The capital budgeting process is one of the most significant aspects of managerial decisions. Since the capital expenditure decisions are more complex and generally involve a huge amount, any decision in this regard will have a long-term effect on the economic health of the enterprise. It is, therefore, essential to make a careful analysis by the top level management before making a profit plan for capital expenditures. An inadequate attention towards capital additions may result in over-investment or under-investment. Therefore, the adoption of a systematic procedure and time table is essential for an effective planning of capital expenditures. The process of capital budgeting will depend on the size of the firm. The nature and number of projects should also be taken into consideration alongwith their complexity and diversity. Simultaneously, it must be ascertained that its cost should not exceed the benefits to be derived.

---

9. Merit, A.J. & Sykes Allen, *Capital Budgeting and Companies Finance*, London, Longreen Ltd., 1973. p. X.

The policy guideline is the most important aspect of capital budgeting because the success of any such proposal depends upon it. The policy guidelines facilitate the translation of long-range plans or mere immediate objectives of a company into specific capital expenditure proposals. They are the most useful in larger firms where size often leads to conflicting divisional objectives. The policy guidelines should not only be specific enough to ensure companywide adherence to policy but also be general enough to permit flexibility, imagination and initiative to flourish at operating levels. There are two types of guidelines, the long run and the short-run. The long-run guidelines relate to top management's future objectives which could be translated into a general statement concerning the physical growth objectives of the firm. It is further spelt out in terms of specific years, future expectations and market. The firm should try to secure general economic or specific industry conditions envisaged for any kind of long-run objectives of the company which could likely to affect the expenditure planning. On the other hand, the short-run policy guidelines relate to conditions external to the firm as exemplified by competitive activity, economic or technological conditions. They deal with factors such as, sales forecasts, wages and material projections, etc. These guidelines are often prepared co-operatively by budget personnel, company economist and other personnel.

The capital budgeting process involves the following important steps :

(I) Origination of Investment Proposals

The very first step of a capital budgeting process is to generate the idea of various investment proposals. Proposal ideas do not generally crop-up overnight. It requires a careful and well thought out planning within an organisation. The search for capital project is not limited to any one function or group of managers. They often originate from several outside sources and from every corner of the business enterprise, *i.e.*, top management level to the level of workers. "The most workable suggestions for the removal of bottlenecks and consequent capital expenditures relating there to come from workmen and foremen. Likewise industrial engineers and plant staff are apt to develop useful ideas in the course of their daily work."[10] These proposals can be related to add new products to the product line or the capacity expansion in existing product line. A systematic procedure for generating proposal must be evolved so that enough investment proposals may be generated to employ fund in a most efficient manner to get maximum return. In this regard it is important to mention that the concerning responsibility centres can generate such proposals more effectively. The proposal for adding a new product may be initiated from the marketing department which thinks of a better way of utilising ideal capacity. The proposal for replacing an old machine or improving production techniques may originate at the factory level.

(II) Collection of Data

The second important step of capital budgeting is to collect the data concerning an originated project. In the process a list of the proposed investments is prepared alongwith the necessary data to appraise them. The relevant data can be obtained from the past experiences specially in regard to the expansion of a new product line. "The data assembly process is not a routine clerical task to be performed on a mechanical basis. It requires continuous monitoring and evaluation of estimates by those competent to make such evaluations — engineers, accountants, economists, cost analysists and other qualified persons."[11]

(III) Project Evaluation

Capital expenditure proposals must be considered with respect to the cash position of the organisation. Such proposals should be made in the light of its cost and benefits. An appropriate technique should be adopted to judge the desirability of projects in the light of the objectives of the enterprise. Cost and benefits should be measured in terms of cash flows "in the entire capital budgeting procedure, probably nothing is of greater importance than a reliable estimate of the cost savings or revenue increases

---

10. Norton, Frank, "Administrative Organisation in Capital Budgeting," *Journal of Business* Vol. 28, 1955, pp. 291-92.

11. J. Fred Weston and Fngene F. Brighan, *Managerial Finance*, p. 290.

that will be achieved from the prospective outlay of capital funds."[12] The risk associated with the projects should also be taken into account in the.decision process. Although the project can be generated by the concerning responsibility centre in a better way, the evaluation of the projects should be made by the impartial expert personnel. "The members of production department may be interested to have the most modern machine or equipment even if the productivity does not increase. This can affect their estimates of cash flows occuring from the projects. Similarly, the Marketing Manager may be too optimistic and may give incorrect estimates of benefits of new product. It is, therefore, necessary to ensure that projects are scrutinised by an impartial group and that objectivity is maintained in the evaluation process."[13] Further, the time value of money must be recognised to achieve this purpose. Simultaneously, it should also be observed that projects should be ranked correctly by the selected criteria and this should not be discriminatory in choosing certain proposals.

(IV) Project Selection

Allocation among the numerous alternative capital addition proposals and the allocation of resources to them is the central problem of the management. There may be a number of proposals for projects that a firm is able to finance. Priorities should be given to select more promising alternatives having the highest rate of return on investment. The management should consider the following primary factors while approving a particular capital project :

(a) Urgency of project;

(b) Availability of repairs;

(c) Credit facilities and

(d) Investment worth.

Thus, a ranking procedure must be developed to distinguish among the many items that compete for the allocation of the capital fund of the firm. As no standard administrative procedure

12. Welsch Glenn, *op. cit.*, p. 263.

13. Pandey, I.M., *op. cit.*, p. 60.

can be laid down for approving the investment proposals, the screening and selection procedure may differ from firm to firm.

(V) Request Preparation

After a careful screening of the proposed ideas by organisers, the next step is the preparation of a request by the profit centre that initiates the project. This concept is important under the philosophy of profit centres whereby individual managers have a specific responsibility for conceiving, proposing and implementing a proposal that may help in achieving the companies strategic plan.

A request is a document that clearly describes in a logical and systematic manner the project being recommended. It includes both pros and cons of all the key factors that are evaluated in arriving at a decision to clarify the reason behind management's recommendation. It must be realistic as far as possible and convey a true flavour of the project covering both the anticipated opportunities and risks. Further more it should be capable of convincing the reader that all important factors have been considered adequately. "Requests are reflections of. management thinking in vital areas. Consequently they inevitably represent one.. basis on which corporate management evaluate the abilities of profit centre personnel and on which the Board of Directors will apprise the abilities of both profit centre and corporate management."[14]

(VI) Approval of Capital Expenditure Plans

The approval of capital expenditure plans is the most important aspect of capital budgeting. These plans are approved by the different levels of management as per the size and volume of amount involved in the plans. Though the ultimate authority to approve such plans is the top management, to simplify this process, the power of approval of the projects of up to a certain limit can be delegated to the lower management or the concerning responsibility centres. Minor capital expenditures of a small amount may be approved by a factory manager or by a departmental head. For the decisions involving a large sum of outlay, approvals

14. Agrawal, G.D., *op. cit.*, p. 13.

are required at a higher level of management. This also provides an opportunity to Board of Directors to examine the aims of operating management. Furthermore, it enables them to agree upon a programme which works out to the best interest of the owners. Where "adoption of new policies are involved, the Board of Directors would want to take ample time in thoroughly exploring the capital budget before giving final approval or ordering its modification alone, the specific lines."[15]

(VII) Project Execution

After the approval of the capital expenditure plans, the next important step of the capital budgeting is to execute them as per the schedule. It is the responsibility of the Finance Department to schedule payments and acquire funds to meet the expenditures. They should compile systematic records on the uses of funds and equipment purchased with the co-operation of Operation Division. As soon as a major capital expenditure project is authorised and undertaken, cost records must be set by project numbers. This record should provide for accumulation of costs by responsibility and type and for supplementary information concerning the progress of the work. A capital expenditure status report for each project should be prepared at short intervals indicating items with respect to both cost and progress. After completion of the project, the cost records should be compiled and total cost be recorded as an asset. Thereafter a final report on the completed project should be prepared. In this regard one thing is important that in no case the under-expenditure on one project should be set off against the excess budget of other projects without the formal approval of top management.

(VIII) Follow up Action

Under the follow up action, a constant and regular evaluation is required for certain projects after their completion. It determines whether the project is producing the expected results or not. It is important because "the follow up comparison of actual performance with original estimates not only ensures better forecasting but

15. Hill, Horace, G. Jr., Capital Expenditure Management, *Journal of Business*, Vol. 28 (1955), p. 288.

also helps sharpen the techniques for improving future forecasts."[16] The basic purpose of a follow-up action is to have an effective control over the capital expenditures for which it is essential do to maintain a clear cut distinction between major and minor capital expenditures. For the control of the major capital expenditures, a systematic procedure should be developed to evaluate the performance of projects during and after completion. So far as the control of the minor capital expenditures are concerned, this can be effectively made by the accumulation of actual expenditures and comparison with budgeted expenditures on a monthly basis. For this, there should be a close co-ordination between the finance department and operational departments. Further, it must be ensured that outlays do not exceed the amount authorised for the purpose.

(XI) Post Completion Audit

The major problem, that is very often encountered on capital budgeting decisions is the poor quality of input data used to support an investment proposal. This can be reduced to a great extent by subjecting all major investment projects to an audit by a term of individuals for the profit centres and departments. "A post completion audit of the earning performance of the capital investment is necessary to preserve the integrity of the estimates of projected earnings and to provide an experience base for improving such further estimates."[17] The post completion audit also helps to make the persons involved in the projection of projects more alert.

(XII) Retirement or Disposal of Investment Proposals

The last step of capital investment decision is to retire the proposals not giving a required rate of return in their liquidation value. According to Joel Dean, "Management responsibility for an investment project ceases only when the facilities have been disposed of."[18] Thus, it is the responsibility of departmental heads to frequently take stock of the situations as to which project is

16. Pandey, I.M., *op. cit.*, p. 61.

17. Dean, Joel, *Measuring the Productivity of Capital*, p. 122.

18. Dean Joel, *Measuring the Productivity of Capital*, p. 288.

to be sold or abandoned. Such steps can be taken before or after economic life of the projects is over, if the projects fail to yiald the required rate of return.

Determination of Investment Worth

Determination of investment worth is the most important factor which is considered at the time of ranking of capital expenditure proposals. The major capital addition should be accorded a special analysis management evaluation and judgement to determine their investment worth. In capital budgeting decisions, the decision-makers face a number of problems such as a choice amongst a large number of alternative proposals, physical and financial interrelationship among these proposals, *i.e.,* complementary or substitute nature of the proposals, financial and non-financial constraints on capital resources, critical manpower problem, unreliable or incomplete data, uncertainties regarding the true risk-return relationship, etc. among the projects. Each of these problems requires a special consideration and may impose different constraints on the investment decisions. It is, therefore, essential to use a sound appraisal method in the determination of investment worth of the proposal. Any method, which is used for the purpose, should be capable of distinguishing acceptable and non-acceptable proposals and should provide a ranking of projects in order of desirability. It should also be able to solve the problem of choosing one from among alternative projects, and should provide a suitable criterion applicable to any conceivable investment project.

The following are the important approaches and techniques being used in determination of investment worth :

1. Pay-back Method
2. Average Rate of Returns Method
   (a) Average Return on Investment
   (b) Average Return on Average Investment
3. Discounted Cash flow Method
   (a) Net Present value
   (b) Internal Rate of Return

Pay-back Method

The pay-back method is one of the most popular methods of evaluating investment proposals. "One of the most popular and widely recognised traditional methods of evaluating investment proposals is the pay-back period. It is the number of years it takes a firm to recover its original investment from net cash flow."[19] Further, it can be defined as the number of years required to recover the original cash outlay invested in a project. This method is easy to apply and more useful in projects with faster pay-backs having more favourable short-run effects on earning per share. The pay-back periods can be computed by the following formula :

P = I/OC

P = Pay-back period

I = Initial incremental amount invested

OC = Uniform annual incremental cash inflows.

The pay-back period of invested amount can be found out by substituting the above mentioned formula into the following imaginary illustration given for acquiring a new machine — Type-A :

(i)	Cost of Machine - A	Rs. 60,000
(ii)	Expected useful life of the machine (non-residual value)	10 Years
(iii)	Earnings and costs over the whole economic life period of the machine :	
	(a) Average annual earnings	Rs. 24,000
	Less : Depreciation @ 10%	Rs. 6.000
	Earnings subject to Income Tax	Rs. 18,000
	Less : Income Tax	Rs. 9,000
	(b) Net Average annual; Earnings	Rs. 9,000
(iv)	Indirect Cash Inflow per annum (Earnings & Depreciation)	Rs. 15,000

19. Weston, F.J. and Brigham, E., *Managerial Finance*, Hinsdale, I, Hinois : The Dryden Press, Holt-Saunders International Edition, 1981, p. 403.

From the above mentioned figure, the pay-back period of the machine-A can be calculated as below :

P = I/OC

P = 60,000 / 15.000 = 4 Years

Thus, the whole amount of investment proposal will be recovered in four years.

If the cash inflow from operations is not uniform, the pay-back period will be calculated in the following manner :

Illustration

Cash outlay required for the proposed project is Rs. 40,000.

Anticipated cash inflows during the four successive years are Rs. 16,000, 14,000, 8,000 and 6,000 respectively.

In this case, the pay-back period will be calculated by adding the inflows of the years. The total cash inflows in first three years are Rs. 16,000 + 14,000 + 8,000 = Rs. 38.000. Further, Rs. 2,000 is still needed to recover from the fourth year. The pay-back period for Rs. 2,000 will be

Rs. 2,000 × 12 months / 6,000 = 4 months.

Thus, the pay-back period for the invested amount will be 3 years and 4 months.

Use of Pay-back Method in Ranking Projects

If the firm has to select one from among two or more mutually exclusive projects, this pay-back method can be used to rank the most preferable one. If the pay-back period calculated for a project is less than the maximum pay-back period set by the management, it would be accepted if not it would be rejected. Thus, it is easy to rank the project according to the pay-back period. The project, which has the shortest pay-back period, is given the highest rank. The lowest rank is given to the project with the highest pay-back period. This can be illustrated by calculating pay-back periods with the help of the following informations :

Cash outlay required for each of the following projects is Rs. 20,000.

Cash inflows from the operations of each project is estimated below :

	Cash Inflows (in Rs.)			
Year	*Project A*	*Project B*	*Project C*	*Project D*
1	5,000	2,500	5,000	2,500
2	5,000	3,500	4,500	3,500
3	5,000	4,000	4,500	4,500
4	5,000	3,000	3,500	4,500
5	—	5,000	2,500	5,000

Further the standard pay-back period is 5 years.

From the above mentioned information, the pay-back period of Projects A, B, C & D can be calculated as under :

Pay-back Period for Project A = Rs. 20,000 / 5,000 = 4 years.

Pay-back period for Project B = (Rs. 2,500 + 3,500 + 4,000 + 3,000 + 5,000) = Rs. 18,000 is recovered in five years.

Thus Rs. 2000 is yet to be recovered.

Pay-back Period 2,000 / 8,000 × 12 months = 3 months.

Thus, the pay-back period = 5 years 3 months.

Pay-back Period for Project C = (Rs. 5,000 + 4,500 + 4,500 + 3,500 + 2,500) = Rs. 20,000 is recovered in five years.

Thus, PBP of Project C = 5 years.

Pay-back Period of Project D = (Rs. 2,500 + 3,500 + 4,500 + 4,500 + 5,000) = Rs. 20,000 is recovered in five years.

Thus, PBP of Project D = 5 years.

On the basis of the above mentioned calculation, it can be analysed as — (i) Project B is not acceptable as its pay-back period is more than the standard period. (ii) Projects A, C and D are acceptable as their pay-back period is within the standard period. (iii) the pay-back period of Project A is shorter than the period of projects C and D. Therefore, in ranking decisions, the Project A will be given the highest rank.

Limitations of the Pay-back Method

The pay-back method is easy to compute and understand. Yet it has some fundamental weaknesses. It does not measure the profitability of the investment worth.

The pay-back method does not consider the time-value of money. In the above example, the pay-back period of the Projects C and D is the same. Hence, each appears equally desirable. However, the money value of the present year is worth more than the money value of the next year. So Project C with its faster cash in flow is certainly more desirable than Project D but this factor is ignored.

It does not distinguish the alternatives having different economic lives. For example, there is an alternative proposal to have the machine of Type-B with identical costs and return as to the machine of Type-A though the Type-B machine has an estimated useful life of twenty years instead of ten years of Type-A. In this situation, the two machines would have about the same pay-back period, however, the alternative machine would be a better one to buy since it may generate double income.

"Despite these deficiencies, the pay-back method is the most widely used. Perhaps the most effective application of the method is as a rough test to determine whether further investigation is warranted".[20]

This method is generally useful in the following cases : (i) precision is not decisive; (ii) the available alternatives are to be screened on a preliminary basis; (iii) cash and credit are crucial and (iv) proposals involve a higher risk.

Average Rate of Returns Method

This method removes the shortcomings of the pay-back method mainly in regard to cash flow. "The accounting rate of return was developed to take care of the drawbacks of cash flow of the pay-back period. It is the ratio of the profit (net accounting

20. Welsch, Glenn, *op. cit.*, p. 366.

depreciation) to capital."[21] This method comprises the following two methods :

(i) *Average Return on Investment*

The average annual rate of return to the investment is calculated through the following formula of this method :

RI = EC/I

RI = Average Return on Investment

EC = Annual Cash Inflow

I = Net Investment Outlay.

Average return on investment can be obtained by substituting the figures shown in illustration as given below :

Ec = Rs. 15,000 I = Rs. 60,000

RI = Rs. 2,000/60,000 = .25 × 100 = 25 per cent

Since, this method is the reciprocal of the pay-back method, all the limitations of pay-back approach are inherent in this method also. Besides this, the fatal weakness that a user may be inclined to compare the result with other incomparable interest rates because of the time value of money and averaging factors. As this method is based on averages, constant earnings over the projects life are assured. Mathematically, it can be demonstrated that the result will always exceed the actual rate of return. For these reasons, this method is not very advisable for use.

(ii) *Average Return on Average Investments*

In this method, the rate of return on investment is calculated to the average investment. The concept of this is, therefore, identical to the above one. The following formula is used to calculate the average annual rate of return.

$$\frac{EC}{I/2} = Ra$$

EC = Annual Cash inflow or cost savings.

I = Net investment outlay.

Ra = Average rate of return on average investment

21. Merret, A.J., and Sykes, Allen, *Capital Budgeting on Company Finance*, p. 95.

Thus, Ra = Rs. 15,000 / 60,000 / 2 = Rs. 15,000 / 30,000 = .5 × 100 or 50 per cent.

Since the initial investment outlay decreases periodically, it is divided by two from which the average balance of the investment is derived. This computation assumes that each annual cash inflow recovers a proportionate part of the original investments. The fundamental weakness of this method is that it does not consider the time-value of money (besides all other drawbacks of the previous one).

Rule of Accept or Reject

As an accept or reject criterion, this method will accept all those projects whose ARR is higher than the minimum rate established by management and will reject those projects having ARR less than the minimum rate. This method ranks a project as number one if it has the highest ARR and the lowest rank is assigned to the project with the lowest ARR.

Discounted Cash Flow Method

The time value of money is the most important factor of the investment worth. The discounted cash flow method is based on the concept that money received today is more important and preferable to money received at some future date. In this regard, Mr. Maclean states, "funds on hand today can be invested in profitable projects and thereby yield additional funds to the investing company. Funds to be received at some future date cannot be profitably invested until that time, and so have no earning power in the interim."[22]

The previous two methods *e.g.*, Pay-back method and Average Return Rate method do not recognise the time value of money at all, therefore, these are not widely used even after they are easy to calculate and understand. The discounted cash flow method fully recognises the time value of money. In this method, all future values are discounted to the present so that comparable values may be added, subtracted and compared. Due to recognition

22. Mackean, John, G., How to Evaluate New Capital Investment, *Hawrard Business Review*, 1958, p. 69.

of time value of money, this method is more preferable for evaluating major capital expenditure proposals. "Because the discounted cash flow method explicitly and routinely weigh the time value of money, it is the best method to use for large-range decisions.[23]

The present value and cash flow are two fundamental concepts that are focussed in discounted cash flow method. Factors, that affect the present value of money, are the rate of interest, the time period. and compounding intervals.

With the help of the following formula the present value of money (to be in future) can be found out :

$$PV = F\left(\frac{1}{1+i}\right)^n$$

PV = Present value

F = Future sum of money

i = Interest rate per period

n = Number of periods.

The present value of money can be obtained by substituting the following problem in the above formula :

Illustration

Find out the present value of Rs. 1,00,000 to be received after one year (hence), if the rate of interest is assumed 10 per cent.

$$Pv = Rs.\ 1{,}00{,}000\left(\frac{1}{1+.10}\right)^1$$

= Rs. 1,00,000 × 0.9090909

= Rs. 90,909.09

The interest of Rs. 90909.09 @ 10 per cent will be

Rs. 90,909.09 × 10/100 = Rs. 9,090.909

value after one year (hence) = Present Value + Interest

Rs. 1,00,000 = Rs. 90,909.09 + Rs. 9,090.91

Rs. 1,00,000 = Rs. 1,00,000

Proved

23. Charles, T. Horngren, *Cost Accounting*, 1976, p. 454.

Thus, the present value of any sum to be received in future can easily be obtained through this method. For this purpose the annuity table can be used to minimise the computation process.

The discounted cash flow method comprises the following two methods :

(1) The Net Present value Method.

(2) Internal Rate of Return Method.

(1) The Net Present Value Method

NPV method is used to calculate the present value of an investment proposal by finding the present value of the expected net cash flows of the proposal discounted at the cost of capital and by subtracting the initial cost outlay of the project from it. "The NPV method is a process of calculating the present value of cash flows (inflows and outflows) of an investment proposal, using the cost of capital as the appropriate discounting rate and finding out the net present value of substracting the present value of cash outflows."[24] A minimum desired target rate of return is required for the discounting purpose. The cash flows are discounted at this rate of return for the periods involved. Thereafter, the amount of present value outlays is compared with the amount of present value inflows. The net present value inflows can be positive, equal or negative. If the net present value is positive, the earning capacity of the project will be more than the minimum rate of return and if it is negative, this will be less than the minimum rate. Accordingly, if the NPV is positive, the proposal will be accepted and if it is negative, it will be rejected. If two projects are mutually exclusive, the one with the higher net present value should be selected.

The NPV can be calculated with the help of the following formula :

$$NPV = [F_1/(1+k)^1 + F_2/(1+k)^2 + ... F_n/(1+k)^n] - I$$

$$= \sum_{t=1}^{N} Ft/(1+K)^t - I$$

24. Pandey, I.M., *op. cit.*, p. 70.

Here F_1 and F_2 and so forth represent the net cash flows. K is the marginal cost of capital. I is the initial cost of the project and N is the expected life of the project.

$\sum_{t=1}^{N}$ Signifies "sum-up" or add the present value of n profit terms.

The concept of NPV can be easily understood by substituting the following illustration in the above mentioned formula :

There are two projects, X and Y having the initial cost of Rs. 1,00,000 each with an average annual cash flows of Rs. 20,000 and Rs. 18,500 respectively. The required rate of return is assumed 10 per cent. The useful life of both the projects is ten years. The NPV of both the projects is calculated as follows :

Table of NPV of Projects X and Y

(Rs.)

Projects	*Average Annual Cash inflows*	*P.V. factor at 10 per cent*	*Net Cash inflows*	*Initial Cost of the Projects*	*NPV of the Projects*
Project-X	20,000	6.145	1,22,900	1,00,000	22,900
Project-Y	18,500	6.145	1,13,683	1,00,000	13,683

Thus, from the above table, it is clear that the present value of projects X and Y is positive, therefore, both the proposals are acceptable. Further the NPV of Project X is more than the NPV of Project-Y, therefore, Project-X is more preferable when both the projects are mutually exclusive.

The NPV approach is popular because it recognises the time value of money and considers all cash flows over the entire life of the project in its calculation. In spite of these merits, this method also suffers from various shortcomings. The method presupposes that the cost of the capital is known whereas it is quite difficult to measure the cost of capital in practice. The method may not also give a satisfactory result when the projects, being compared, involve different amount of investments. Projects, requiring a large investment, may not be diserable even with a higher NPV. It may also mislead when dealing with alternative proposals having different life periods. The proposal with a higher NPV may involve longer economic life to the point that it should be less preferable to an alternative having a shorter life.

2. Internal Rate of Return Method

This is another technique of the discounted cash flow method in which the time value of money is considered. This method is also stated as a yield of an investment, marginal efficiency of capital, rate of return over cost and time adjusted rate of return, etc. The internal rate of return (IRR) is defined as the "interest rate that equates the present value of the expected future cash flows or receipts, to the initial cost outlay."[25]

In contrary to the Net Present Value Method, this method determines the discounted rate of return that the proposal will generate. The exact rate is found to discount the future inflows in such a way that can equalise the discounted sum to the sum of outflows. The concept of this approach is based on "the rate of return that a project earns is that rate of interest that will discount the future cash earnings of the asset so that their sum exactly equal the present value of the cash investment in the asset."[26] In other words, it is the rate at which the net present value of the investment is zero. It is called internal rate because it depends solely on the outlay and proceeds associated with the project and not on any rate determined outside the investment.

The equation for calculating the internal rate of return is :

$$[F_1/(1 + r)^1 + F_2/(1 + r)^2 + \dots\dots\dots\dots F_n/(1 + r)^n] - I = O$$

$$= \sum_{t=1}^{N} F_1/(1 + r)^t - I = O$$

The F_1, F_2 represent cash inflows in successive years, F_n represents cash inflows in the last year, I is the cost of

25. Fred Weston and Eugene, F. Brighan, *Managerial Finance*, 1977, p. 295.

26. Welsch, Glenn, *op. cit.*, p. 374.

investment proposals, n is the expected life of the proposal, 'r' is the internal rate of return that is to be determined at which the Net Present Value (NPV) is zero. The value of 'r' cannot be computed directly, therefore, it is found out by trial and error. In this approach, any rate of interest is selected to compute the present value of cash inflows. If the calculated present value of the expected cash inflows is lower than the present value of cash outflows, a lower rate should be tried. On the other hand, a higher rate should be tried if the present value of inflows is higher than the present value of outflows. This process is continued unless the net present value becomes zero.

There may be two distinct situations under which the internal rate of return is to find out.

(i) When the amount of cash inflows is equal in each year.

(ii) When the amount of cash inflows is not equal in each year.

Both these situations can be illustrated with the help of the following example :

There is an investment proposal of Rs. 60,000 for the purchase of the Machine-A with no residual value. The expected life of the machine is 10 years and an equal annual cash inflow is Rs. 15,000. The estimated earnings is 15 per cent.

By substituting the above data in the following equation, the present value of an annuity of Rs. 15,000 a year for 10 years.

$I/F = PVIF_a$

I = Investment

F = Annual Cash Inflows

$PVIF_a$ = Present value of interest factor of annuity.

$PVIF_a$ = Rs. 60,000/15,000 = 4.0

4.0 is the relevant factor of PV Annuity table. The present value of Re. 1 received annually for 10 years (expected life) is referred and discount factor closest to 4.0. By going through the annuity table, it is found that the 4.0 falls between 20 per cent (4.192) and 22 per cent (3.923). Therefore, by trial and error process as shown in the following table. We can ascertain that the rate of return is approximately 20.6 per cent = 21 per cent

Discount Rate	*Discount Factor (Drawn from Annuity table)*	*Cash Inflow Per annum (Rs.)*	*Present Value of Total Cash inflow (Rs.)*
20 per cent	4.192	15,000	62,880
22 per cent	3.923	15,000	58,845
21 per cent	4.0534	15,000	60,801

(a) Difference in discount rate = 1 per cent

(b) Difference in present value of total cash flows at the rate of 20 per cent and 22 per cent = (62880-58845) = 4035

(c) Difference of present value at a discount rate of 22 per cent from the original investment = 62880-60,000 = 2880

Therefore, the rate of 20 per cent will be adjusted as follows :

$$\frac{2880}{4035} \times 100 = 0.565 \text{ per cent}$$

20 per cent + 0.565 = 20.565 per cent or 20.6 per cent approximately.

22 per cent – 0.565 per cent = 21.435 per cent

At the expected rate of return of 15 per cent, the proposal can be expected because its internal rate of return is 21 per cent which is higher than the expected rate of return.

In the second situation, where the cash inflows are not equal in each year, the calculation of Internal Rate of Return can be illustrated with the following example :

Cost of the Project Rs. 1,50,000

Residual value = 0

Expected useful life = 5 years

Annual cash inflows :

1st year = Rs. 50,500, 2nd year = Rs. 45,500

3rd year = Rs. 40,500, 4th year = Rs. 35,500 and

5th year = Rs. 30,500

Expected cost of capital or rate of interest is 10 per cent.

On the basis of the above given information, the first rate for trial is selected, *e.g.*, 15 per cent. At this rate, the discount factor is obtained from the annuity table for each year and the sum of present value is found out.

(In Rs.)

Year	*Estimated cash inflows*	*Discount factor drawn from Annuity table of PV @ 15 per cent*	*Present value*	*Discount factor from PV Annuity table @ 14 per cent*	*Present value*	*Discount factor from PV Annuity table @ 12 per cent*	*Present value*
1st	50,500	0.870	43,940	0.877	44,290	0.893	45,100
2nd	45,500	0.756	34,400	0.769	34,990	0.797	36,260
3rd	40,500	0.658	26,650	0.675	27,340	0.712	28,840
4th	35,500	0.572	20,310	0.592	21,020	0.636	25,580
5th	30,500	0.497	15,160	0.519	15,830	0.567	17,290
Total	**2,02,500**		**1,40,460**		**1,43,470**		**1,50,070**

Since the sum of discounted cash flows, is less than the cost of project which means that the selected trial rate, *e.g.*, 15 per cent is too high. Therefore, this trial process is repeated at 14 per cent and 12 per cent respectively. The second trial at 14 per cent is also too high. The third trial at 12 per cent equates approximately the initial cost of the project with the sum of the present values of the earnings for five years. Therefore, the proposed rate of return is 12 per cent. This proposal is not acceptable as the rate of return is less than the expected earning rate.

Both the methods of discounted cash flow are theoretically sound as the most important element of investment worth, the time value of money is fully recognised in these approaches. Besides, they also take into account the other necessary aspects of an investment proposal like the inflows and out-flows of money, the estimated useful life of the projects and the required capital expenditures, etc. Therefore, these methods are much preferable to previous methods like pay back and average rate of returns method, in spite of the involvement of a huge and difficult computation process.

Although there are some common factors that are involved in both the Net Present Value and Internal Rate of Return Methods, there is a difference in both the approaches regarding selecting or accepting the projects. The NPV method accepts all independent projects whose NPV is greater than Zero. And ranks mutually exclusive projects by their NPVs. On the other hand, the IRR method calls for accepting independent projects, where IRR is greater than the cost of capital, and for selecting among mutually exclusive projects having the higher IRR.

But these differences are also only structural that lies on equations of both. All the values in the equations are identical except for r and k. Further, it can be seen that if r>k, then NPV> o. Accordingly, both the methods give the same result to accept or reject decision for specific projects. If a project is acceptable according to the NPV approach, it will also be acceptable if the IRR method is used. However, under the following conditions, the NPV and IRR methods can rank a project differently :

1. If the cost of one project is larger than the cost of other one.
2. If the timing of cash flows of the projects differ.

Both the IRR and NPV methods have some distinct advantages. The IRR method avoids the arbitrary choice of a minimum rate of interest and the true interest rate generated by the proposal is computed. On the other hand, the NPV method avoids the detailed trial and error method of searching for the rate, so in case of uneven cash inflows it can be applied easily. However, the IRR method is more widely used.

The role of judgement must not be overlooked in using the results of the various evaluation techniques of capital budgeting. Since all the evaluations are based upon the estimates of future potentials, the results cannot be better than the estimates. Besides, the other important factor, the factor like moral of employees also influences the proposals. These factors cannot be quantified but can be an overriding factor in the decision process. The role of management judgement and experience still looms large despite the mathematical results obtained through techniques.

The process of controlling of capital expenditures can be summarised as below :

1. A capital expenditure manual should be prepared. This should state the procedures to be followed in all matters

2. The clearcut distinction should be made in between the revenue expenditures and capital expenditures based on the nature of fixed assets.

3. The forms of authorisation of capital expenditures must be designed.

4. The capital budgeting should be integrated with the budgetary control system so that all aspects of budgeting may be considered. Particularly the forecasting and budgeting of cash should be taken into account and linked up. with the capital needs.

5. An adequate record of each fixed asset over its useful economic life should be kept so that the experiencc gained on running costs, repairs, depreciation and profitability may be used for future capital expenditure projects.

6. To deal with the sanctioning of projects, a capital expenditure committee should be set up. Responsibility for authorisation, showing which projects require approval at board level and which can be approved by the lower management without ratification from a higher authority should be fixed.

All these factors should be considered in the light of nature and size of a particular business concern dealing with all essential relevant data.

5

Budgeting — Some Observations

The importance of sound budgetary system was amply emphasized by the Administrative Reforms Commission (ARC) in its report on Public Sector Undertakings, long back in the year 1967. The Administrative Reforms Commission observed that "An effective mechanism of financial management and control can be built up only on a sound budgetary system. The budget of a public enterprise has not only to serve the requirements of external accountability and internal control but it has also to provide a plan of action, a framework in which to review progress and a standard against which to review performance."[1]

Thus, even in public sector it may be stated that budgeting is the backbone of the effectiveness of being an enterprise. It has been aptly remarked that "the financial performance of an enterprise depends significantly on how the use of its resources is planned and controlled. In other words, budgeting is the key to productive financial planning and control. Public enterprise in our country have shown scant regard to this most important management tool while planning their physical and financial targets."[2]

If one looks at the scenario of the Indian Public Sector Undertakings, one gets the view that except for a few of the larger undertakings, most of the public enterprises had not switched over from the traditional budgeting till the sixties. This

1. *ARC Report* : Public Sector Undertakings, 1967, p. 56.

2. Mishra, R.K. *Budgeting in Public Enterprises*, published in *Management* in Government Journal of the Department of Personnel and Administrative Reforms, Vol. XIV, No. 4. January-March, 1983, p. 401.

position remained almost the same for a long time. Prof Mishra amply clarifies this position when he says "Till the end of the Sixties, Public enterprises mostly prepared very short budgets which broadly comprised a revenue budget and ways and means statement........ thus, the coverage and the type of budgeting did not meet the ends of performance and business budgeting."[3]

Here it may be concluded that though our public sector undertakings reached the stage of "traditional budgeting from the stage of no budgeting, much was still to be done to make the performance of those undertakings more and more effective."[4] The Committee on Public Undertakings observed this fact and suggested the Government to make it obligatory for the public sector undertakings to prepare detailed budget estimates. The Government accepted the suggessions but "most of the public enterprises continue to follow the traditional pattern of forms and procedures."[5] Therefore, the Administrative Reforms Commission recommended in its report that "Public Undertakings should prepare comprehensive budget to embrace the entire Organisation and to cover interalia the following range of budgeting activities.

(a) Production Estimates

(b) Sales Estimates

(c) Cost of Production Budget with its necessary sub-divisions, *e.g.*, :

— Materials Purchase Estimates;

— Labour and Personal Estimates;

— Overhead Estimates;

— Plant Maintenance Estimates.

(d) Manpower Budget;

(e) Township and Welfare Estimates;

(f) Research and Development Estimates;

(g) Capital Expenditure Budget;

---

3. Mishra, R.K. *op. cit.*, p. 404.
4. Chaubey, A.N. Unpublished Thesis 'Budgeting in Public Enterprises.'
5. Laxmi Narayan, *Principles and Practices of Public Enterprise Management*, New Delhi, 1980, p. 360.

(h) Profit & Loss Estimates;

(i) Cash Flow Estimates;

(j) Capital Employed Budget — Fixed and Working Capital."[6]

At the same time, to make it more effective, the Committee on Public Undertakings emphasised to prepare realistic budgets and presented its observation in its statement in their 15th Report on Financial Management in Public Undertakings....... "The committee feel that if the units concerned are asked to prepare their own budgets, they will be more realistic because they will be prepared by persons with first hand knowledge. Moreover, the units will feel more responsibility for adhering to the estimates. The Committee recommended that the system of concerned unit preparing its own budget may be adopted by all the public undertakings. The budgets of the units will ofcourse have to be approved by the Board of Directors at the Head Office."[7]

Besides the preparation of the realistic budget, it was also observed that there should be an effective budgetary control system to monitor the budgetary provisions with actual performance and can be reported to the authorities concerned for which the sound Management Information system should be developed to channelise it.

Apart from the above remarks, the Administrative Reforms Commission and the Committee on Public Undertakings have also passed special comments from time to time on the management of some of the important aspects of the functioning of Public Sector Undertakings in India which are closely related to the cost of capital expenditures of the projects and cost of production and integral part of budgeting-process. These aspects may be enumerated as Construction Management, Production Management and Material Management A brief discussion of all these follows :

Management of Projects under Construction

The Administrative Reforms Commission and the Committee on Public Undertakings have not only put many observations

6. ARC : Report on Public Sector., *op. cit.*, p. 57.

7. Government Policy for the Management of Public Enterprises, *op. cit.*, p. F-64.

regarding on-going public sector undertakings, but have also put some special comments on the projects under construction. The Committee observed that cost over-run is the main problem for the new projects. "High escalation in costs is the result of delay in the construction of the project, cost over-run and loss of production for several months in the initial period."[8] The estimates prepared for the public sector projects in a number of cases have never been prepared in time and realistically with the result that they have to be revised frequently. The Committee on Public Undertakings stated that the "Estimates should be prepared in time and sent to the Government for its approval before the expenditure is actually incurred. Estimates should be understood in its literal sense and should not be equated to actuals after the money has been spent."[9] Further while studying the detailed Project Report of various projects, the Committee on Public Undertakings noticed that the aspects covered 'in the reports varied from project to project. Some of the detailed Project Reports did not even include the capital outlay, manpower requirements, location of sites, source of raw materials, etc. of projects...... "The Committee felt that no report should lack basic informations such as the cost and profit estimates, manpower requirements, source, cost and consumption of raw materials, etc."[10] In the interest of proper execution of the projects and to obviate the chance of omission of important aspects from such reports, the committee recommended that "the Government should evolve a standard checklist of items which should invariably be included in the Detailed Project Reports."[11] Further in pursuance of the suggessions of the committee, the then Dy. Prime Minister and Finance Minister, Mr. Morarji Desai suggested in a letter addressed to the Ministers of Industrial Development and Company Affairs that, "the question of improving the planning of industrial and mining projects in the public sector and of streamlining the

8. Khanna, K.K., *Management of Public Sector Enterprises in India*, 1988, p. 52.

9. Committee on Public Undertakings (3rd Lok Sabha) Report p. 22.

10. Gadhok, D.N., *Accountability of Public Enterprises to Parliament*, Sterling Publications Pvt. Ltd., 1980, p. 95.

11. Gadhok, D.N., *op. cit.*, p. 95.

procedures for examination and sanction in any ministry, has been engaging my attention for sometime. The criticism, that has been voiced in many quarters of the low returns earned by the public sector plants, could have been avoided to considerable extent if there has been a better understanding of the economics of investment proposals at the time of approvals given to them."[12] Further he drew the attention towards some deficiencies in planning and appraisal process. ... "Inaccurate and generally exaggerated estimates of demand, lack of attention to the problems of economic location, plant size and product mix, inadequate appreciation of the importance of estimating outlays and incomes, overtime and the absence of any real analysis of the benefits and costs of projects to the economy as a whole are some of the deficiencies in project planning and appraisal."[13] The Committee on Public Undertakings drew the attention towards the mode of assessing the feasibility and preparation of Detailed Project Report as suggested above in the words...... "Feasibility studies and Detailed Project Report should not only help the government to avoid the sort of mistakes in planning projects that have occurred so far, but also lesser administrative delay among the various ministries."[14]

Production, Planning and Control

In most of the public sector undertakings, the-production has been far behind what was envisaged and far below of their installed capacity. It not only leads to locking-up of scarce resources but also results in widespread economic repercussions in linked industries and heavy avoidable imports. The perennial under-utilisation of production capacities has also the effect of inflating the costs of production and adversely affecting the financial results of the undertakings. On the one hand, the public sector enterprises were not completing their utilisation capacities and, on the other hand, it was found that there was also a tendency to fix the production targets lower than their rated capacity. In this regard, the Committee on Public Undertakings

12. *Ibid.*

13. *Committee on Public Undertakings (4th Lok Sabha) Report-48*, pp. 39-40.

14. Khsnna, K.K., *op. cit.*, p. 78.

has observed that....... "there is an inherent tendency on the part of the enterprise to fix annual targets at a level which is much lower than the attainable capacity or rated capacity."[15] The need for sound production, planning was felt to remove all these deficiencies and to achieve a better financial result. In this regard, the Bureau of Public Enterprises (BPE) has instructed various ministries from time to time to advise public sector Undertakings under their control to examine and review their existing production control organisation and system in the light of factors such as change in market standard of performance and quality pattern of market demand, production diversification, product development and prototype manufactures, etc. without impairing their long-term objectives and with a view to establishing close co-ordination between marketing,, and production on the one hand and production and management on the other.

Material Management

Efficient utilisation of inventory is essential to earn returns in terms of higher productivity and level of customer's service. A lower level of inventories runs the risk of stock-out and a higher level runs the risk of obsolescence and avoidable increase in cost. Therefore, an economic balance is essential to be struck between the cost of carrying inventories and the cost of a desired level of customer service. But the Public Sector Undertakings in India have not paid much attention to maintain equilibrium between these two and they have been suffering with a high level of inventory *i.e.* up to fifteen month's turnover. In this regard, the Committee on Public Undertakings has observed that "some undertaking have been carrying inventories as high as fifteen month's turnover. Holding of such a high level of inventories cannot be justified."[16] Further the Committee observed that the reduction of levels of inventories from fifteen months to six months of turnover would release enough capital which would be gainfully used in the same undertaking or for financing some other important projects.

15. Khanna, K.K., *Ibid.*, p. 78.

16. Khanna, K.K., *Ibid.*, p. 93.

The position may be summed-up as "Though our public enterprises have progressed to an identifiable degree in respect of budgeting and budgetary control, there is still a scope for improvement to make budgeting more effective as a tool of forecasting, controlling and decision making in the hands of those concerned with the fate of the enterprise."

6

Profit Planning and Control — A Survey of Selected Public Sector Undertakings

This study includes a detailed observation on profit planning and control in public sector steel industry with special reference to Bokaro Steel Plant, an integrated unit of Steel Authority of India Limited (SAIL), *i.e.*, steel industry in public sector, it is, therefore, in the fitness of things to limit the discussions and observations to the undertakings either influencing the steel industry or undertakings comparing with steel industry (in terms of their nature size and investments). Thus, a few undertakings, that have been selected for the purpose are :

(i) ITI, Naini, Allahabad (Communication Sector)

(ii) MECON, Ranchi (Consultancy & Service Sector)

(iii) CCL, Ranchi (Energy Sector)

(iv) HEC, Ranchi, TSL, Naini & BPCL, Naini
(Some selected units of Heavy Industries)

A brief discussion of their budgetary practices follows :

To see the budgeting-process of an enterprise with a critical eye, it is relevant to have a brief introduction of the enterprise so that an appropriate picture of its purpose, nature, size and activities may be had in mind.

INDIAN TELEPHONE INDUSTRIES (ITI), NAINI, ALLAHABAD

Introduction

Indian Telephone Industries, Naini is a subsidiary unit of the Indian Telephone Industries Limited under the Ministry of Communication, Government of India. The corporate office of the company is at Bangalore in Karnataka. The Naini Unit was established in 1971 at Naini (Allahabad) with an objective to strengthen the country in the field of electronics and communication. The main products of Indian Telephone Industry, Naini are solar panel, telephone equipments, MARR system, Multi-channels, communication systems and optical fibres, (Digital system) etc.

Budgeting Process in Indian Telephone Industries, Naini

(i) Initiation

The finance Division at the Corporate Office of the company coordinates all activities concerned with the preparation of budget estimates. On receipt of budget targets and instructions from the Corporate Office, unit heads, in turn, issue instructions to all departmental heads/divisional heads under their control to prepare budget proposals. In Indian Telephone Industries. Naini, both Revenue and Capital Budgets are prepared in prescribed formats as given in Budget Manual :

(i) Revenue Budget (Operating Budget)

Operating budget of the company consist of the budget estimates for the following :

1. Sales-and Service Budget
2. Production Budget
3. Material Budget (Commitment and expenditure)
4. Personal Budget
5. Ways and Means Budget
6. Budgeted Profit and Loss Account and Balance sheet

The corporate office holds a meeting of all the unit heads to discuss and finalise the proposed plan for the ensuing budget year for each unit based on the following important factors :

(a) Available orders in hand,
(b) Market conditions with reference to future demand,
(c) Government policies,
(d) Available infrastructure,
(e) Available technology in international markets.

Thus, keeping in view the above mentioned factors, the corporate management fixes the target for each unit. Accordingly, the Indian Telephone Industries, Naini gets the target for the budget year as fixed by the corporate office. Thereafter, the Production Planning and Control Department of the unit starts the budgeting-process at the unit level.

The budget estimates for all operating activities are prepared by the department concerned showing the revised estimates for the current year and budget estimates for the budget year. It is prepared in both physical and financial terms. The revised estimates for the current year are based on actual performance of the first six months of the year and expected performance for the remaining months. Further it is broken into a month-wise target. A brief note is furnished indicating the reasons for variations between the actuals of the previous year and the revised estimates for the current year together with the revised estimates of the current year and budgeted estimates for the budget year.

(ii) Capital Budget

The budget estimates for capital expenditures are prepared under two main heads, *viz.*, (a) New Projects and (b) Continuing Projects/Schemes.

The budget estimates are prepared both under 'commitment' and 'expenditure'. An item is said to have been committed when the purchase orders are placed or contracts are entered into. 'Expenditure' implies actual outflow of cash.

The current year's budget estimates for capital expenditures are reviewed with reference to the actual performance for the first-six months and revised estimates for the current year are formulated.

2. Budget Approval

A comprehensive budget for all operating activities and capital expenditure is sent to the corporate office in a consolidated form by the end of October of each year for its approval. The Board of Directors approves the budget with slight modifications (if required) and communicate to the unit concerned by the end of March for its implementation.

3. Monitoring of the Budget

Once the budget is approved by the Board, it is sent to the units concerned. The budget section of the Indian Telephone Industries, Naini unit communicates it to various responsibility centres for closer monitoring and control of performance. Each of the manufacturing division and service centre makes a reporting with respect to a monthwise actual performance against the budgeted performance in physical and financial terms. These reports are reviewed by the management. The reasons for significant shortfalls are identified and corrective measures are taken.

4. Standard Norms

In Indian Telephone. Industries, Naini, the standard norms have been fixed for the following :

(a) Inventory Norm : Materials required for minimum two months in case of in-land items and three months in case of abroad purchases.

(b) Work-in-progress : One month of production.

(c) Stock in trade : Two weeks of the sale.

(d) Debtors : Two months.

(e) ABC Analysis :

A 70 per cent of value 10 per cent items,

B 20 per cent of value 20 per cent items,

C 10 per cent of Value 70 per cent items.

METALLURGICAL AND ENGINEERING CONSULTANTS (INDIA) LIMITED (MECON), RANCHI

Introduction

MECON, Ranchi is mainly a Job (Service) Industry under Public Sector Undertakings in India. It offers the total consultancy covering planning and analysis, feasibility and project reports, basic and detailed engineering, construction and project management, erection and commissioning, etc. The head office of the unit is at Doranda, Ranchi in the Bihar State of India. It also has other offices at New Delhi, Calcutta, Hyderabad, Bangalore, Bhilai, Bokaro, Rourkela, Durgapur, Madras, Vishakapatnam, Mangalore, Bamnipal, Korba, Balasore, Tiruchirapally, Tirunelvelli, Okhla, Gurgaon, Bombay, Dehradun, Kanpur and Udaipur.

MECON is a specialist in the steel sector and has contributed a lot to the development of the iron and steel industry in India and abroad through consultancy services and interactive transfer of appropriate technologies. MECON commences a whole spectrum of disciplines, experiences and the know-how to adopt technologies to suit the needs of not only India but of other developing countries as well. It offers in-plant training in operation as well as in-house training in design and engineering.

MECON has engineered five integrated steel plants in India. It masterminds greenfield steel plants based on coke-ovens-blast Furnace — Basic Oxygen Furnace — Primary Mill-continuous Casting — Finishing Rolling-Mills with all auxiliary and ancillary facilities, Mini and Midi Steel Plants, Alloy and Special Steel Plants, expansion and modernisation of existing steel plants and associated infrastructure. It offers projects on a turnkey basis involving design of equipment and systems including supply, errection and commissioning for Hot and Cold Rolling Mills for Ferrous and Non-Ferrous Metals/Alloys for flat and non-flat products, processing lines, Tube Mills and Pipe Plants, Coal Carbonisation and by-product plants, coverter Gas Cooling, Cleaning and recovery plants, Blast Furnace modernisation etc.

Though MECON is a specialist in steel, it is also providing valuable services to the other sectors. It is using its skill to engineer chemical and refractory industries, non-ferrous industries (aluminium, copper, lead and zinc), cement plants, engineering shops and material handling plants. It has also made contributions to geology, mining, mineral, engineering, defence production, power generation, general engineering and project management.

MECON is also providing consultancy services to other developing countries, *i.e.,* Abu Dhabi, Algeria, Bangladesh, Dubai, Indonesia, Liberia, Nigeria, Sharjah, Syria, Vietnam and Zimbabwe, etc. To stream line the works undertaken abroad, it has offices in Russia (MOSCOW), Nigeria (Lagos, Warri and Ajaokuta), the U.S.A. (Pittsburgh and Warren) and West Germany (Dusseldorf). It has access to state-of-the-art technology through collaborations with specialist companies in France, Italy, Japan, Norway, Switzerland, the U.S.A., Russia and West Germany. MECON has an ongoing programme on technology update through its own Engineering Research and Development (ERD) Wing situated at the Head Office, Ranchi.

Budgeting in MECON

In MECON, the budgetary process starts in the month of June every year and is completed by the end of August. The Organisation has its Accounts Manual which contains the budget manual also. The Budget Committee prepares all the budgets by comprising all the information and feedback from different sections and departments through their departmental heads. Budget estimates are planned in the light of the Memorandum of Understanding signed with the Steel Ministry by the Organisation. The budget is finalised by the Board of Directors. Before the finalisation of the budget, the figures are moderated, if necessary, in the light of the Memorandum of Understanding. Then it is sent back to the centres concerned for implementation. The budgeted figures are compared with the actual performance on a monthly basis. Proper corrective measures are taken in regard to any negative deviation on actual side.

Types of Budget Prepared in MECON

The Finance and Accounts Department of the Organisation prepares Revenue and Capital Budgets.

Revenue Budget

Revenue Budget constitutes the budget estimates for both receipt and payment.

Receipts

The receipt side includes the expected income from the business sources as well as the non-business sources. The business sources include the estimated receipts from both the service and project sectors. The budget for service sector is prepared on the basis of an expected income. The ratio of the budgeted income between service sector and project sector is about 45 per cent and 55 per cent.

Payments

The revenue budget for the expenditure side is prepared in the light of the budgeted income. It includes the estimated amount of fixed expenditures and variable expenditures. Variable expenditures plan includes the expected payments for sub-contracts as well as vendors of the company.

Budget Technique

The company incorporates both the techniques in regards to preparation of revenue budget, *i.e.*, historical budgeting and performance budgeting.

(a) Historical Budgeting

The budget for fixed expenditures is prepared on the basis of past experiences and figures. It is assumed that no much more changes take place in regard to the fixed expenditures. Therefore, the figures are adjusted with a slight changes as per the current needs and the concerned budget is prepared.

(b) Performance Budgeting

The technique of performance budgeting is used to prepare the budgets for revenue and expenditure sides both. On the revenue side the income from the project sector is estimated and it is compared with respect to the actual performance. For the expenditure side also the same procedure is followed.

Since the MECON is imparting only consultancy services and

indulges in the design engineering works, therefore, the revenue budget does not include the production plan and sales plan on physical line.

Capital Budget

The capital budget of the company includes the plans for planned capital expenditures and non-planned capital expenditures. Capital budget for planned expenditures is based on the Planned Capital Report which is supported by the internal resources as well as extra budgetary support. The extra budgetary support includes the governmental budgetary support It is prepared on need basis.

CENTRAL COALFIELDS LIMITED (CCL), RANCHI

Central Coalfields Limited (CCL) is a subsidiary unit of Coal India Limited (CIL) which was established on 1975 with the purpose to streamline the management of the public sector coal industry. The company CIL was formed with the following five subsidiary companies :

1. Eastern Coalfields Limited (ECL) located at Sanctoria (West Bengal).
2. Bharat Coking Coal Limited (BCCL) located at Dhanbad (Bihar).
3. Central Coalfields Limited (CCL) located at Ranchi (Bihar).
4. Western Coalfields Limited (WCL) located at Nagpur (Maharashtra).
5. Central Mine Planning & Design Institute Ltd. (CMPDIL) located at Ranchi (Bihar).

Further three more subsidiaries were formed under this. These are Northern Coalfields Limited (NCL) Singrauli (MP), Mahanadi Coalfields Limited (MCL), Sambalpur (Orissa) and South Eastern Coalfields Limited (SECL) Bilaspur (MP). Thus, at present CIL has eight subsidiaries. It falls under the Department of Coal, Ministry of Energy, Government of India.

The Central Coalfields Limited (CCL) covers Bokaro, Ramgarh and Karanpura Coalfields of Bihar. Besides these, some smaller coalfields like Hutar, Daltanganj and Giridih (all located in Bihar) are also included in it.

The Headquarters of CCL is located at Ranchi which controls eleven production areas and a sales office located at Calcutta. Besides these, one Central Workshop and one Central Store are situated at Barkakana near Ranchi. There are several collieries and washeries in the area covered by the company. The company is managed by a Board of Directors headed by a Chairman-cum-Managing Director.

Nature of Operation

The nature of operation in a coal industry differs from a manufacturing unit. The industry possesses some special features as narrated below :

(i) In a coal industry the product is not processed form inputs to outputs but the raw coal extracted from mines is termed as the final product. The original form of coal (product) is neither improved nor altered by men and machines.

(ii) The industry has two types of mines. One is open-cast mines and the other is underground mines. The open-cast mines involve less time and funds to make them operative whereas the underground mines require more time and money under the revenue and capital heads during the course of their development.

(iii) In the industry, additional funds are required till the coal reserve of a particular project is not exhausted whereas in a manufacturing unit, once the construction project is over, the need for additional funds becomes limited.

(iv) Geological factors are much more important in a coal industry because a coal mine can be workable only when it is found favourable in the sense of geological conditions, whereas in a manufacturing unit, this cannot be treated as a much more accountable factor in the production process. Thus in the coal industry a return on investment may not be as it is planned earlier.

(v) Once the coal is extracted from a mine, it cannot be

preserved safely for a longer period because the quality of coal starts deteriorating within a few months.

(vi) In comparison to manufacturing units, the mining projects require an investment of heavy funds at the starting time because from the very beginning of the development of a mining project, all the machines and incidental services are needed to be maintained.

(vii) As the operation of a mine depends on geological conditions which cannot be foreseen, the requirements of machinery and equipments cannot be forecast as accurately as in case of the manufacturing companies.

(viii) In the coal industry, the standard cost system is not applied for the accounting of operational costs same as applied to manufacturing units. It is so because the operational costs in any particular mine depend on a very large number of continuously changing interdependent variable factors like geological conditions, mining methods, inputs status, etc.

(ix) If a particular mine is abandoned, the amount invested in it becomes worthless and is put under a total loss.

Estimation of Coal Reserves

The Geological Survey of India is an agency to make a tentative estimate of the reserves of coal in the country and to also identify the areas where these reserves are located. The CMPDIL examines the estimates in detail and if it feels that the property of coal is marketable and infrastructure is available, then it goes for a detailed exploration with regard to the depth, thickness and quality of coal and the process of geological faulting, folding etc. Thereafter a report is prepared and is placed before the competent authority for approval. After the approval, the report is submitted to the concerned Regional Institutes of CMPDIL (Asansol, Dhanbad, Ranchi and Nagpur). The Regional Institute prepares the Feasibility Report on the basis of standard norms with respect to the method of mining, manpower, plant and machinery required, land and building, life of project, capital improvement requirements, cost of production, selling price and profitability, etc. The Feasibility Report is put up before the

Board of Directors of the company for its approval and after its approval, it is forwarded to CIL, Energy Ministry and Finance Ministry for concurrence. Once the project is sanctioned, the necessary process with regard to land acquisition, power supply, procurement of plant and machinery, building, deployment of manpower etc. is started. The Feasibility Report is modified from time to time during the course of its implementation. For such modifications a project report is prepared and revised based on the progress shown after one or two years as per the current needs of the operation. The project report is also duly approved by the Board of Directors and the Ministry concerned.

Budgeting in Central Coalfields Limited (CCL)

As stated above, the company holds some special features in regard to its nature of operation. Therefore, the budgetary techniques applied in a manufacturing unit may not be more suitable and applicable in the same manner in CCL. The inventory system, standard costing system cannot be maintained on an itemwise, productwise and timewise in the coal company. Consequently, the variance and cost control techniques are also not applicable in a centralised manner. But the types of budgets prepared in CCL are almost the same as to the manufacturing units. A brief discussion on budgeting in CCL is presented below.

Coordinating Agencies

In central Coalfields Limited, the Management of Finance is under the control of a Director (Finance). At the area level, the Area Finance Managers have been deployed to control the financial activities of the concerning area. For the purpose of budgetary control, the budgets for the ensuing budget year are prepared in CCL every year. The financial performance is reviewed on a regular basis in which a special emphasis is given upon controllable costs areas.

Since all important functions relating to extractions of coal from mines and its management are performed by the area offices located at the various points of the widely spread mines, these offices play a very important role in estimating and initiating budget proposals.

The Finance Department of CIL also provides staff service for the evaluation and monitoring of financial performance of its subsidiaries. It also co-ordinates the budgeting-activities and assists in the financial appraisal of large projects and central purchase transactions. In accordance with the approved budgetary provisions and priority of emerging needs of the subsidiaries, the CIL channelises the funs obtained from the Government.

Types of Budget

In CCL, both revenue and capital budgets and prepared in a comprehensive form.

I. Revenue Budget

The Revenue Budget of CCL comprises mainly the budget estimates for the following functionaries :

1. *Production Budget*

The production budget is prepared both in quantitative as well as monetary terms. First of all, the Headquarters fixes the production target for each area based on the previous years figures. Thereafter, the area-management decides the production estimate for the budget year based on the actual result of the last year, subject to the adjustment of other conditions prevailing at that time. Keeping this in view, after going through a detailed discussion at the area level, the unitwise production estimates are finalised and incorporated into a compact form. The budgeted quantity is translated into a monetary form by the finance department of the area concerned. Thus, a detailed production budget for a particular area is prepared and forwarded to the Headquarters. By incorporating the production budget estimates of all the areas, a comprehensive production plan is prepared at the headquarters, level, matching with the production target of the budget year. With respect to the policies and commitments of the company, all necessary adjustments are made at the top level management, while finalising the annual production plan of the Company.

2. *Material Cost Budget*

Material is the second important element for which a detailed plan is prepared by the company. Being a company of different nature, materials used in CCL can not be termed as raw materials. They are used to extract coal from mines. The important materials that are used frequently in this process are petrol, oil and lubricants (POL), explosive, heavy earth moving machinery (HEMM) spares and timber. The expenses incurred on these items are included in the material cost budget.

3. *Manpower Budget*

The Manpower is the third important segment of budgetary process in CCL. Mines running under CCL cover not only a very vast area but also involves thousands of workers of different categories at both inside and outside of the mines. At the area level, the Area Personnel Manager is the controlling authority of the manpower employed in that area. The amount spent on their salary, wages and other perquisites is put under the manpower budget.

4. *Coal Transportation Budget*

In CCL, a huge amount is spent on the transportation of coal from the point of extraction to the railway siding. For this the budget is prepared under a separate head.

5. *Miscellaneous Contractual Works Budget*

Other important functions in CCL are the development of infrastructure, repairs and maintenance of mines, roads, buildings and machineries. These are discharged on a routine basis and the expenses incurred on such activities are included in the miscellaneous contractual work budget.

6. *Welfare Head*

A number of welfare activities are operated by CCL for its employees as well as for the people of the mining areas. Under the community development programmes, it provides various facilities like roads, wells, hospitals and schools. It runs dispensaries at each unit level and regional hospitals covering two to three areas. At Headquarters level, it runs a central hospital with all basic facilities and equipments. It also provides some special grants to schools and colleges situated under the area. Thus a large sum is spent on the welfare head and a separate budgetary provision is made for this purpose.

7. *Monitoring of Sale*

The delivery orders of sale are controlled by the headquarters. But the monitoring of the sales/despatches is essential to match it with the sales targets of the company. There are two modes of sale in CCL, one through road transport and the other through rail transport. At the area level, the Area Sales Manager monitors all activities regarding the despatch of coal through appropriate means according to delivery orders.

Thus, in CCL, the budgets are prepared for the above-mentioned important functionaries. By incorporating all these, a comprehensive revenue budget for a budget year is prepared and finalised at the headquarters level. The extensive exercise is made to match the budget with the policeis and goals of the corporate office.

II. Capital Budget

A separate budget under the capital head is also prepared in CCL. The project officers are directed to submit a list of the jobs of capital nature concerning their areas. It includes the capital items required to produce (extract) coal like heavy earth moving machineries (HEMM), other equipments and the cost of builidngs for residential as well as rehabilitation purposes. The expenses incurred on the development of the underground mines are also booked under the capital heads. The areawise capital requisitions are procured and by incorporating all these, a consolidated capital plan is chalked out and finalised at the Headquarters level.

HEAVY ENGINEERING CORPORATION LIMITED (HEC), RANCHI

Introduction

Heavy Engineering Corporation Limited, Ranchi (HEC) was incorporated on 31st December, 1958, with the primary objectives of achieving self-sufficiency and self-reliance in the field of design and manufacture of equipment and machinery needed for iron and steel industry and other core sector industries like coal, mining, railway, etc.

Heavy Engineering Corporation Limited has three manufacturing units, *i.e.* Heavy Machine Building Plant (HMBP), Heavy Machine

Tools Plant (HMTP) and Foundry Forge Plant (FFP), The HMBP manufactures a wide range of equipments like blast furnaces, rolling mills, coke oven, sinter plants, EDT cranes, converter, etc. for steel plants and equipment like wagon tipplers, crushers, excavators, OB drills, draglines and mine winders, etc. for coal mining industry. The HMTP manufactures a complete range of heavy machine tools including CNC machine tools and special purpose machine tools required by Railways and other customers. So far as FEP is concerned, it manufactures various types of non-ferrous, gray iron, SG iron and steel castings, forgings and rods. This unit also acts as a feeder unit to HMBP and HMTP.

Besides the above manufacturing units, HEC also undertakes a comprehensive range of consultancy services by providing feasibility study, detailed project reports, equipment supplies, execution of projects and plants on a turnkey basis from concept to commissionings in various areas, *e.g.*, raw material handling, plants, coal handling plant, coal washeries, low temperature carbonisation and gas treatment plants, sinter plants and CCM plants, etc. through its projects and consultancy division.

Quality Improvement Plan

In pursuance of excellence for quality, Heavy Engineering Corporation had taken up the general awareness programme of ISO Certification and had already received ISO-9001 Certification for its HMBP and HMTP units. Further, the company has acquired ISO-9002 accreditation for its third unit *i.e.* Foundry Forge Plant during the year 1997-98, thereby, making HEC an ISO-9000 company. The overall improvement in performance in HEC and its accreditation to ISO have not only shown a sign of restoring past glory but it have also enhanced the image of H.E.C. as a quality builder of equipments and machineries.

Order Booking

The company has been facing problems in order booking for the last two or three years due to a recession in capital goods market. Though the demand in capital goods market has started improving, liberalisation of imports, entry of multinationals and large domestic industrial houses in the market pose new challenges.

The company is making all out efforts and expects to secure more orders from different sectors like steel, mining, railways, defence. One of the key areas being focussed by the company is to procure orders specially from steel and mining sectors to meet the production targets.

Cost Reduction Measures

Cost reduction measures have been conceived as major thrust areas of the company and all necessary steps are being taken to reduce costs in all areas of operation. A few important areas selected for the implementation of cost reduction measures may be enumerated as under :

(i) Reduction in power and fuel cost,

(ii) Reduction in material cost to achieve the target of net sales fixed by B.I.F.R.,

(iii) Reduction in employment cost by releasing employees under Voluntary Retirement Scheme (VRS) during the year 1997-98,

(iv) Reduction in social overhead cost by leasing out utilised lands/buildings, sub-contracting civil maintenance and horticulture works and rationalising the hospital charges for paying cases in line with the local market rate,

(v) Reduction in power consumption in township through various managerial actions,

(vi) Reduction in rejection level in FFP, MHBP and HMTP and

(vii) Reduction in down time of machines from present level.

Budgeting in Heavy Engineering Corporation Ltd.

The budgeting-process in Heavy Engineering Corporation Ltd. starts in the months of July-August of every year with the receiving of the office memorandum from the Department of Heavy Industry, Ministry of Industry of the Government of India regarding the preparation of plan and non-plan budget estimates for the budget year. The budget estimates are prepared in given formats. The company prepares the Revenue Budget and Capital Budget.

The Management of the Company decides the target of net sales & production of its manufacturing units, *i.e.*, F.F.P., H.M.B.P. and H.M.T.P., as well as the turnkey and consultancy work of the projects.

Based on the order position and expected orders to be booked from the customers during the year and next year, the net sales target and production targets are fixed. Items for the use of internal customers are also manufactured and considered for production target.

The plants chief and finance chief are intimated by the corporate-office about the targets and are asked to prepare a detailed budget estimate in both physical and financial terms.

The same target is sent to the Ministry, Department of Heavy Industries for inclusion in the revised budget estimate for the year and the budget estimate for the next year. The Corporate Office prepares the budget for revised estimates and budget estimates burden (for Bank Interest and Interest on Government Plan Loan and Non-Plan Loan).

The headquarters load, township and social overhead and interest load are transferred to plants for the preparation of profitability statement. As such the units have the impact of corporate overhead social overhead and interest burden on their performance.

Different departments send their proposals to the corporate office according to their needs. The Corporate Finance examine the cases and include them in the budget keeping in view the target and cost factor.

The township and social overhead budget involves the medical facilities, welfare activities including school, sports and other social activities of the organisation. The plants prepare their budget in consultation with the Marketing Department, Production Planning Department, Design Department, Materials Management Department, Maintenance Department and other service wings.

- Based on the production plan, the material budget is prepared keeping in view the Inventory level, (unnecessary blockage of money in inventory is avoided).

- production schedule is drawn and the requirements of different items right from design to material procurement are worked out.
- Despatch schedule is drawn in consultation with PPC keeping in mind the commitment to the customer with respect to the despatch of materials/items.
- The material purchase budget, material consumption budget, production budget, despatch (sales) budget, employment cost budget, manufacturing and other administrative expenses budget are prepared and are incorporated in a comprehensive budget estimate.

Considering the liquidity position of the company and acute financial crunch, the company approaches the government for financial assistance, which, if agreed by the government, is received in the shape of a loan. For capital expenditure, the loan is planned loan and for other expenses it is a non-planned loan. Loans are sanctioned for period of five years and are repayable after completion of the year. The rate of interest for planned loan is 16 per cent per annum normal and 18.75 penal and for a non-planned loan 18.75 per cent normal and 21.25 per cent penal.

TRIVENI STRUCTURALS LTD (TSL), NAINI

Triveni Structurals Limited is a subsidiary unit of Bharat Yantra Nigam Limited controlled by the Department of Heavy Industries under the Ministry of Industry. TSL was set up at Naini, Allahabad in July, 1965 as a joint enterprise of the Government of India and Vercentigite Osgerred Osgerraichiesche Elsemund Stahloworks. AG (VOIEST), Linz of Austria, a public sector company of the Government of Austria. The Company was taken over by the Government of India in 1987. The company is primarily engaged in the manufacture of heavy steel structural products, such as tall towers, mast for power transmission communication, T.V. broadcasting, industrial building, hydro mechanical equipments, pressure vessels, etc. Though the company has made achievements in the areas of marketing, production, technology development, the company is running under a recurring loss. The loss is mainly due to non-materialisation or delayed materialisation of expected orders and acute shortage of working capital, non-availability of matching steel, non-supply of steel by clients, etc.

TSL is mainly a jobbing industry, so the production is started only after getting an order. Orders are procured on a nomination basis. The Sales Department collects the requirements published in newspapers and places before higher authorities to quote tenders. All the concerning departments are asked to furnish relevant information regarding the tenders. The Sales Department compiles the data and presents before the higher authorities to determine the winning price. The tenders are finalised by the top level management of the company and are submitted to the customers. The tenders are supported by the relevant information regarding technical and financial aspects which can arise during the delivery period.

Budgetary Process in TSL

Once an order is obtained from the customer, the budgetary process starts. The Sales Department prepares a budget for the job, considering the figures supplied by the different departments to obtain the job under various heads, *i.e.*, electricity, labour, overhead, consumable inputs, raw materials, etc. The Engineering Department of the company calculates the quantity and determines the quality parameters. The Production Department estimates the labour cost to be incurred. Considering all these aspects, a job to job-budget is prepared by the Sales Department. The Sales Department sends the budget proposals to the budget section of the Finance Department. The Finance Department gives a thorough look upon the estimated budget proposals and incase of any shortcoming it is referred to the concerning department for necessary modifications. Thereafter a consolidated budget proposal is sent to the Board of Directors for approval. As soon as the proposed project is taken for execution, the material indents are sent to the Purchase Department. The Purchase Department processes the indents to purchase the items. Before placing the orders for the purchase of the items they are tallied with the bugetary provisions. If any variation is found with the actual cost on the higher side, the reasons for such as increase are recorded and justified. If it is compensated by an other item, it is also mentioned. The approval of the Managing Director is must for any change on the higherside. The company also prepares the profitability statement showing budgeted profit and loss account

Monitoring of the Budget

The targets with respect to work in-progress is compared with the monthwise actual performance. The Board of Directors review the progress quarterly. For this purpose two special sessions are organised at the middle of the year and at the end of the year. In these special sessions, the causes of variations are found out and corrective measures are taken.

BHARAT PUMPS AND COMPRESSORS LIMITED (BPCL), NAINI

Bharat Pumps and Compressors Limited is also a subsidiary unit of, Bharat Yantra Nigam Limited. The company was established in 1970 at Naini, Allahabad as a Government of India enterprise. The company is engaged in the manufacture of fluid handling equipment for supplies to oil exploration and exploitation sector, fertilizers, chemicals and other process industries, thermal and nuclear power plants, refineries and pipelines, etc. The manufacturing range of the company includes centrifugal pumps, reciprocating compressors, reciprocating process pumps, sucker rod pumping units, cementing units and various types of gas cylinders, ammonia, chlorine and dissolved acetylene gas cylinders. The company is manufacturing these products based on the know how acquired from the leading manufacturers of the world and has established itself as a prime supplier of these products in the country.

Budgeting in BPCL

The company is guided by the Budget Manual regarding the preparation of the operative and capital budgets. This prepares the budget estimates for each important aspect of its operating activities, *i.e.,* sales budget, production budget, overhead budget, raw material consumption budget, personnel budget, budgeted profit and loss statement, etc.

The Planning Department of the company collects Information relating to Production Budget from the concerning Production Departments. On the basis of these information, the Planning Department prepares quantitative budget estimates and sends it to the Finance Department for compilation. The Finance Department prepares a comprehensive revenue budget by incorporating the budget estimates of other functionaries. The consolidated budget is sent to the Board of Directors which approves it with necessary adjustments and sends it back for implementation. The Company also prepares the performance budget in prescribed formats as required by the department of Heavy Industries, Ministry of Industry, Government of India. The performance budget is sent to the department concerned. The Performance Budget comprises a detailed informations regarding budgetary provisions, item-wise production performance showing actual figures of the previous year and the budgeted estimates for the ensuing budget year. It also contains figures showing progress of schemes under execution and particulars of new schemes to be taken up during the budget year. The Performance Budget also includes figures showing operational results of the company in monetary terms and unit cost data analysis.

To have an effective budgetary control over the period of its application, the budgeted figures are compared with the actual performance and variance analysis is made by the Planning and Development Department of the company. The company has been giving more thrust upon cost reduction schemes for the last few years.

7

Profit Planning and Control in Public Sector Steel Industry — With Special Reference to Bokaro Steel Plant (BSL)

Before we embark upon a detailed study of Profit Planning and Control (budgeting) in the Bokaro Steel Plant, it would be worthwhile to present in brief the development of Public Sector steel industry in India.

The Industrial Policy Resolution of 1948 and 1956 assigned a significant role to the public sector. The policy resolution of 1948 envisaged a greater role for the state in the economic development of the country. Under this, the responsibility for setting up new undertakings was reserved in the state in six basic industries, *i.e.* coal, iron and steel, aircraft manufacture, ship building, mineral oils, manufacture of telephone, telegraph and wireless apparatus. The scope of public sector was further expanded in Policy Resolution, 1956.

The then Prime Minister of India, Pandit Jawaharlal Nehru, firmly believed that rapid industrialisation was the only panacea to the economic ills of the country. He was convinced that the industrialisation ultimately depends upon heavy industries with 'steel' as a base. He was a stout champion of the cause of steel industry. The First Plan period was decisive in laying down the firm foundation for the establishment of steel industry in the Public Sector in India. The earlier efforts of the government had amply borne out the rising demand for steel in the wake of the emerging industrial picture of the country. The Iron and Steel (Major) panel had placed the steel demand at about 3 million tonnes by the end of 1960. Hence, there was an urgent need to set up fresh capacity of steel in the country.

At the suggestion of the World Bank, the Government appointed a technical mission in 1952 to assess the existing and future demands of steel in India. Since the Government was in a hurry, it decided to go ahead with the setting up of an integrated steel plant in the public sector at Rourkela without waiting for the report of the Commission.

Rourkela Steel Plant

The first step in the direction of a public owned steel plant was taken with an agreement between the Government of India and West German Combine Krupp, Dunaz, signed in December, 1953. The agreement provided for the setting up of an integrated steel plant at Rourkela, with an initial capacity of 5 lakh tonnes of steel at an estimated cost of Rs. 9.5 crore. A preliminary report was received from Krupp-Demag in May, 1954 and was followed by a detailed project report in January, 1995. Later on it was decided to 'increase the plant capacity to one million tonnes.

In pursuance of the agreement, the Hindustan Steel Limited (HSL) was formed on 19th January, 1954 as a private Joint Stock Company under the Indian companies Act 1913. The company was assigned the task of construction and management of Rourkela Steel Plant. The combine was to contribute Rs. 9.5 crore to the share capital so as to have a representation on the Board of Directors. Later on the government took over the share of the company in December, 1956.

In the meantime, the report of the Technical Mission constituted for assessment of the demand of steel was received. The Mission estimated the demand of 6.0 MT of ingot steel for the country by 1960-61, corresponding to about 4.5 MT of finished products-demand. The existing capacity of ingot steel was much lower than the demand that revealed a gap of about 4 MT between the projected demand and actual capacity. This led the government to the urgency of establishing more steel plants in the country.

Bhilai Steel Plant

The Government of India and the USSR entered into an agreement on 2nd February, 1955 for the establishment of a steel plant at Bhilai. The initial capacity of this plant was one million tonnes of ingot steel. It was for the first time that the Soviet Union was venturing on a big scale beyond the boundaries of the Socialist Block.

Durgapur Steel Plant

The third big iron and steel plant in the public sector was set up at Durgapur in West Bengal with the assistance of the United Kingdom (U.K.). "The cost of the project was estimated as Rs. 115 crore as against the estimated cost of Rs. 128 crore for the Rourkela Steel Plant and Rs. 110 crore for Bhilai Steel Plant."[1]

The Bhilal and Durgapur steel projects were under the direct control of the Ministry of Iron & Steel. In the meantime, the re-examination of India's administrative system particularly of industrial and commercial enterprises was under consideration with the Government. In this regard, Paul H. Appleby had submitted his report in 1956. Appleby recommended that "There should be a presidential movement of consolidation of all special organisations, according to a scheme of coherent mission."[2] The government accepted this view and as a consequence the Bhilai and Durgapur projects were merged with HSL on 1st April. 1957. Thus, HSL was assigned the task of construction and management of all three steel plants of the public sector. These were Rourkela Steel Plant at Rourkela (Orissa), Bhilai Steel Plant at Bhilai (MP) and Durgapur Steel Plant at Durgapur (W.B.).

Commissioning of Steel Plants

The much awaited moment of commissioning was an event of great jubiliation in the history of public sector steel plants. Dr. Rajendra Prasad, the then President of India, lent his dignity with the inauguration of iron production at Rourkela on 3rd February, 1959 to be followed by the Bhilai Steel Plant on the

1. Government of India, *Planning Commission*, Second Five Year Plan, p. 396.
2. Srinivasan, N.R., *The Corporate Story of SAIL*, 1990 p. 38.

very next day *i.e.* on 4th February, 1959. From 1960 onwards, it was a period of hard toil to ensure an integrated operation and achieve rated capacity production. The Bhilai, Rourkela and Durgapur steel plants functioned as the three units of the HSL till 1972. It ceased to exist with the formation of Steel Authority of India Limited (SAIL) in January, 1973.

Bokaro Steel Plant (BSL)

The Ministry of Iron and Steel directed HSL to take preliminary steps for the establishment of Bokaro Steel Plant in 1957. This was the fourth Public Sector steel plant of India established with foreign assistance.

"The Bokaro Steel Limited was incorporated as a new Private Limited Company on 29th January, 1964 with an authorised capital of Rs. 1000 million."[3] The company was assigned the task of the construction and management of Bokaro Steel Plant. Further, an agreement was signed on 25th January, 1965 Between the Governments of India and the U.S.S.R. for the financial and technical assistance from Soviet Russia. The first phase of 1.7 MT was completed with the commissioning of the third Blast Furnace on 26th February, 1978. The BSL functioned as a separate company under the direct control of Ministry of Iron and Steel till April, 1978. It became an integrated steel plant of SAIL under the Public Sector Iron and Steel companies (Restructuring) and Miscellaneous Provision Act, 1978 passed on 1st May, 1978.

Steel Authority of India Limited (SAIL)

The formation of SAIL in 1973 was an important land mark in the history of Public Sector steel industry of India. During 1972, there was a serious thought at the government level on the need for a suitable structure for the public sector steel industry for a faster development. The Government sent a delegation under the leadership of Sri Mohan Kumarmangalam, the then minister for steel and mines, abroad to study the organisation of governmental enterprises notably in the U.K., France and Italy. On 10th January, 1972, the Government approved the proposal

3. Srinivasan, N.R., *The Corporate Story of Bokaro*, Published by SAIL., 1988, p. 16.

for the establishment of a holding company for public sector and associated input industries.

The Steel Authority of India Limited (SAIL) was formally incorporated at New Delhi on 24th July, 1973, with an authorised capital of Rs. 2000 crore.[4] The shares of the HSL, HSCL, BSL, Salem Steel Plant, BCCF and NMDC were transferred to SAIL and they became its subsidiaries. At present SAIL consists of the four integrated steel Plants, e.g., Bhilai Steel Plant (BSP), Durgapur Steel Plant (DSP), Rourkela Steel Plant (RSP), Bokaro Steel Plant (BSL) together with the two special steel plants — Alloy steel Plant (ASP) and Salem Steel Plant (SSP). Besides these, the central units of R & D Centre for Iron and Steel (RDCIS), Central Marketing Organisation (CMO), Raw Materials Division (RMD), Growth Division (GD), Environment Management Division (EMD), Central Coal Supply Organisation (CCSO), Centre for Engineering and Technology (CET) and Management Training Institute (MTI) are also the constituents of SAIL. It also owns subsidiary companies — Indian Iron & Steel Co. (IISCO) Burnpur, Maharashtra Electrosmelt Limited (MEL) and Visveswaraya Iron and Steel (VISL). The corporate office of SAIL is located at New Delhi.

The Steel Authority of India accounts for 12.4 MT of ingot steel capacity in public sector steel industry. At present it ranks tenth among the top steel producing companies of the world. "Today SAIL is one of the largest corporate entities in the country, with an investment of around Rs. 11,000 crore. Its innate strength lies in its technologists and professionals and a trained manpower of two lakh and a sales turnover of more than Rs. 10,000 crore."[5]

SAIL is headed by a chairman, who is of the rank of secretary to the Government of India, and has a full time Board of Directors. The chief Executive of integrated steel plants are the members of the Board that has a full control over the affairs of the company.

---

4. Srinivasan, N.R., *The Corporate Story of SAIL,* published by SAIL 1990, p. 89.

5. Dr. Hariharan, *Background Paper on SAIL.*, p. 1., 1995, MTI, Ranchi.

Network of SAIL

Being the largest corporate entity in steel sector, SAIL has a very vast net work throughout India to achieve its targets. Its constituent steel plants, subsidiaries, branch sales offices, fertiliser cells, stockyards and shipping offices are spread over the country.

Growth of Investment in Steel Industries under Public Sector

In the light of the rising demand for steel and steel technologies in the country, many new projects relating to steel industry have been undertaken by the Government in the last few years. Alongwith this, massive modernisation programmes are also undertaken in various steel plants under the MOUs signed between the Government and SAIL. All these have accounted for a huge investment with a growing trend in public sector steel industries in India. The following table shows the investment growth in this sector from 1982-83 to 1993-94.

TABLE 7.1

Investment in Public Sector Steel Industry

(Rs. in Crores)

Year	*Investment*
1982-83	5149
1983-84	5719
1984-85	6329
1985-86	6763
1986-87	6913
1987-88	7100
1988-89	7437
1989-90	8300
1990-91	16217
1991-92	18249
1992-93	19282
1993-94	20846

Source : *Public Enterprises Survey*, 1993-94 Vol. I. p. 6.

Being the largest entity with such a huge investment, it is imperative to make a detailed study of profit planning and control (Budgeting) in public sector steel industry. As this, sector covers a very vast area, the Bokaro Steel Plant one of the important integrated steel plants of SAIL, has been undertaken for this purpose.

Profit Planning and Control (budgeting) in BSL

As an operating company, Steel Authority of India Limited is empowered to prepare a comprehensive budget for all its constituent units, keeping in view the market demand and market strategy of saleable products, the corporate office fixes targets for its subsidiaries based on Memorandum of Understanding signed with the Ministry of Steel. Thereafter every production unit prepares an Annual Performance Plan (APP) to match the commitments in the Memorandum of Understanding for the year. This plan is finally approved by the Board of Steel Authority of India Limited. The detailed discussion on the budgetary practices in Bokaro Steel Plant are as under.

1. Objectives of Budgets

As ultimately everything hinges on an effective financial performance for the success of a company, it is explicitly stated in the objectives of SAIL that it should be run on a commercial line. It implies that the cardinal yardstick of profit is the touchstone of a successful endeavour. Keeping in view the profit motive of the operating company (Steel Authority of India Limited), the Bokaro Steel Plant prepares its budget on a commercial line. For this purpose, all important aspects of performance budgeting are adopted here. A micro level planning is essentially needed for each and every aspect of operational and non-operational activities by involving all the components and responsibility centres to maximise the gross margin. The aim of the budget is to project profitability by exhibiting the amount of expenditure to be incurred at the level of planned output as well as corresponding revenue at that level of production.

2. Nature and Properties

The Bokaro Steel Plant is one of the largest steel plants with an expanded capacity of 4.0 MT ingot steel. In such a large complex, targets cannot be achieved unless a micro level planning for all its important as pects is made. The budget prepared in Bokaro Steel limited has the following main properties :

(a) Commercial Budget

The aim of the budget in Bokaro Steel Plant is to project profitability by exhibiting the amount of expenditures to be incurred to achieve the set production target as well as the corresponding revenue at that level of production. Based on the planned expenditures, the standard cost of production of each of the product, by-product and services as well as engineering shops is also calculated. As cost is directly related to profit, the cost control and cost reduction policy are strictly followed in Bokaro Steel Plant.

(b) Customer Oriented Budget

A customer oriented budget is prepared in the Bokaro Steel Plant. A prime importance is given to the customer satisfaction from both the angles, *i.e.*, quantity as well as quality. BSL has two types of customers namely internal customers and external customers.

(i) *Internal Customers*

The production flow of BSL, as given on the following chart, shows the process of production of various units :

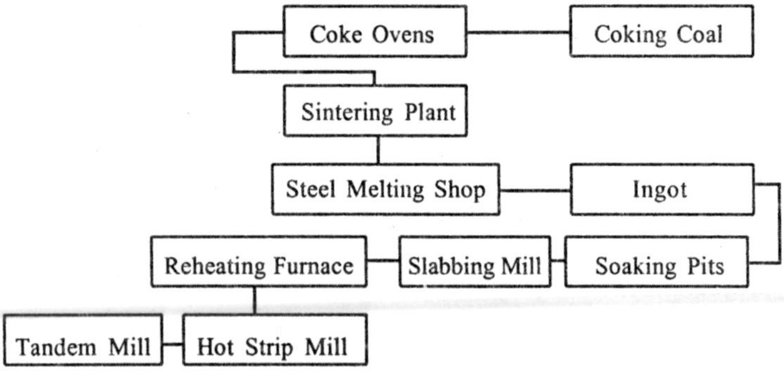

The above mentioned chart shows clearly that one unit is producing inputs for the other units and shops of the plant. The raw coke is obtained from coke mines and put into coke ovens. The coke produced in coke ovens is used in sinter plant in which it is converted into an excellent charge material. This charge material is used in blast furnaces to produce hot metal which is used as an input in steel metal. The steel metal is used as input is steel melting shop to produce ingot steel. The ingot steel is used as an input in slabbing mill to produce slabs. These slabs are used as an input in hot strip mill where it is converted into hot rolled coils and hot rolled plates. Further, these are used in cold rolling mill to convert it into cold rolled coil, C.R. sheet, G.C. sheet and G.P. sheet. Thus, all the units are linked together and one is a customer for the other units. In BSL the budget is prepared with a view to satisfying the need of its internal customers.

(ii) *External Customers*

The market-customers are treated as external customers. The pig iron saleable steel, C. R. sheets, G. C. sheet and G. P. sheets are the finished products of the plant which are sold in the market for external customers. The projection of demand of its product mix is made by the Central Marketing Organisation (C.M.O.) of Steel Authority of India Limited. The final shape of the production plan is given in the light of the projected demand in tune with the Memorandum of Understanding signed by the Corporate Office. This plan is matched with the requirement of external customers with respect to cost, quality and time factors.

(c) Micro Level Planning and Control

The budget prepared in Bokaro Steel Plant incorporates all sorts of planning and control for each and every aspect of operational and non-operational activities. The effect of any movement or diversion on overall profit is calculated and planned in such a way which can give maximum result at a minimum cost. A special attention is given to traditional areas, *i.e.,* re-utilisation of components and spare parts to effectively implement the cost reduction and cost control plan.

(d) Self Commitment

This is the most effective part of the budgeting in Bokaro Steel Plant. Here decisions are not thrust by the top level management, rather each centre of functionaries makes its own commitment by fixing a standard norm of output in a given time to match it with budgetary targets. Thus it also becomes a responsibility of the respective centres to give the committed results. To strengthen the self commitment programme, the quality circles system has been introduced at various centres of the plant. A group of' people working together form a quality circle consisting of 8 to 10 members. At present about 18,000 employees of the Plant are covered under this scheme.

(e) Root Level Involvement

In Bokaro Steel Plant the budget proposals are initiated at the grassroot level. Based on these proposals, a comprehensive budget of the Plant is shaped after an extensive exercise and thorough discussions. The discussions are made at the various sections and departments under the leadership of sectional and departmental heads in which views are shared with the floor level staff. They are also made aware of the importance of cost control, cost reduction and quality control programmes with a view to achieving the set targets and objectives of the plant. Thus, the employees of each and every section feel that they are a part of the commitment made by their section and department towards the final goal of the Plant.

Budget Manual

The Steel Authority of India Limited has its own Budget Manual for all its constituent units. The Budget Manual is of a confidential character. It elaborates the guidelines in detail for preparation of budgets by the unit (Plant) concerned. The manual provides various formats for presentation of different types of budget proposals by the different departments of the unit concerned. The relevant formats provide space (columns) for figures to be inserted relating to the previous year (budgeted and actuals) as well as planned figures for the budget year.

Types of Budgets

The Bokaro Steel Plant has introduced the performance budgeting system in a complete sense. The given Budget Manual is followed in this-respect. The following two types of budgets are prepared in Bokaro Steel Plant mainly :

(i) Operational Budget and (ii) Capital Expenditure Budget.

(i) Operational Budget

The budget is prepared in the form of Annual Performance Plan (APP) under which result oriented budget is prepared by all operational and non-operational shops and departments. The operational budget prepared in Bokaro Steel Plant has a composition of all the departmental and shops budgets who prepare their budgets in quantitative term. Thereafter the quantitative budget is translated into monetary term by the Cost and Budget Section. The operational budget has the composition of the following budgets prepared by the different functionaries in their prescribed formats:

(i) Sales budget
(ii) Production budget
(iii) Raw material budget
(iv) Stores and spares budget
    (a) Procurement budget
    (b) Consumption budget
(v) Inventory budget
(vi) Administrative expenses budget
(vii) Other expenses and provision budget
(viii) Contractual expenditure budget
(ix) Human resource budget
(x) Employees remuneration and benefits budget and
(ix) Miscellaneous deferred revenue expenses budget.

The consolidated operational budget is prepared by the cost and budget section of the Finance Department by incorporating all' departmental operational plans.

(ii) Capital Expenditure Budget

There is a separate Capital Budgeting Section under the finance Department to prepare budgets for planned capital expenditures. The capital budget of Bokaro Steel Plant includes two types of capital items. One is planned capital items and the other one is non-planned capital items. The planned capital items include all the capital expenditures incurred on planned projects. The power regarding investment decisions for the projects of up to a certain limit are delegated to the managing director. For the capital projects, which cost more than the delegated limit, investment decisions are taken directly by the Board of Steel Authority of India Limited. The replacement of machines and equipments, major capital repairs and renovations mainly come under the planned capital expenditures. The non-plan capital expenditures include expenses incurred on non-planned capital items like office furniture and equipments.

Cash Flow Plan

Apart from these two budgets, a rolling plan for quarterly cash requirements is also prepared by the Cost and Budget Section to be sent to the Corporate Office to meet the cash requirements'. The Corporate Office transfers the fund to the account of BSL to meet monthly cash requirements.

3. Co-ordinating Agencies

In Bokaro Steel Plant, there is no Budget Committee as such to coordinate the budget proposals but there is an effective machinery for the preparation, coordination, compilation, assimilation and finalisation of the budget proposals. The following sections and departments act as co-ordinating agencies regarding the budgeting-process in BSL.

Cost and Budget Section

The Cost & Budget Section plays the most important role regarding co-ordination and preparation of operational budgets in a consolidated form. The section runs separately under the Finance Department and is headed by a Dy. Chief Finance Manager (Cost and Budgets). This section is amply equipped with persons having professional expertise and high ranged computers. The section applies updated techniques of management accounting. It works in coordination with the cost control department with regard to budgetary process. The quantitative operational budgets prepared by the various departments are translated into monetary forms by this section. Thereafter it prepares a consolidated budget with the co-ordination of all works and non-works departments. Any shortcoming in the departmental budget proposals are pointed out by the section and accordingly readjustments are made. Apart from this, the section also prepares standard cost sheet, daily profit statement, mid-month report (MMR), last month report (LMR) and management information report to enable the management to make great strides towards planned objectives.

Production Planning and Control & Sales Co-ordination Department

This is another important co-ordinating agency involved in budgetary process. This department prepares a consolidated budget proposal for all works departments in quantitative terms. The sales co-ordination wing of the department co-ordinates between central Marketing Organisation of Steel Authority of India Limited and production units of the plant. The lists of required materials to be despatched to various stockyards and customers are placed by the Central, Marketing Organisation to sales co-ordination wing of the department. Accordingly it makes necessary arrangements for despatches. The department is headed by a general manager (Services) who controls it with the assistance of an assistant general manager (PPC & SC).

Cost Control Department

The Cost Control Department calculates the standard cost of each unit of input and output. A cost control hand book is published by the department for an internal data circulation. The book contains detailed figures relating to the budgeted profit and loss account, budgeted cost of major raw materials and common store item, cost of diversion, consumption budget for stores and spares, sensitivity analysis, item-wise budgeted contribution and net profit. The total operating cost, overheads, depreciation, interest and total cost of production are also shown in the hand-book. The department highlights the cost reduction policies and other information which are important to achieve set goals. This department plays a very important role in making employees aware of the cost control and cost reduction programmes, essential elements for the maximisation of profit. Under the cost control policy, the SAIL has achieved the target of saving of

Rs. 700 crore in 1997-98, out of which the BSL contribution is Rs. 233 crore.

Capital Budgeting Section

The capital budgeting section is also a wing of the Finance and Accounts Department. This section is responsible for preparing a consolidated capital budget for planned capital expenditures with the co-ordination of Technical Investment Cell and Investment Planning Unit (TIC & IPU). This section is headed by a chief finance manager and assisted by junior managers of professional expertise.

Technical Investment Cell and Investment Planning Unit (TIC & IPU)

This department is solely responsible for judging and verifying the technical viability of the projects which come under planned capital expenditures. The departmental head of the concerned capital plan preparing unit, sends its proposal to this department (TIC & IPU). The department verifies the proposals from the point of view of its technical viability and sends its approval to the Capital Budgeting Section for further action. In this context the department also co-ordinates the proposing department, Finance Department, Design Bureau and the Managing Directors Secretariat.

Organisation and Method Department

This department co-ordinates the activities regarding the preparation of budgets for non-plan capital expenditures. The department concerned requiring capital expenditures sends its proposal to Organisation & Method Department for its approval. The Organisation and Method Department verifies the proposals from the point of view of its justification. After being satisfied, it forwards the proposal with its comments to the Finance Department in a consolidated form for its final sanction. This department is headed by an assistant general manager (Organisation & Method).

4. Budgetary Process

Initiation of Budget Proposals

The budgeting process in Bokaro Steel Plant starts in the

month of October of each year to prepare a budget for the budget year. This process is underway with the circular issued from the Cost and Budget Section, Capital Budgeting Section and other co-ordinating agencies, requesting the departmental heads of all works and non-works departments, to submit their departmental budget proposal plan for the coming financial year. There are about 66 works departments and 44 service departments in the Plant. They prepare the budget proposals for their departments relating to the next financial year, *i.e.*, April to March. So far as the operational departments are concerned, the budget proposals for the ensuing budget period are prepared in the prescribed formats regarding their requirements for raw materials, stores and spares, contractual expenditure, non-plan capital expenditure and administrative expenditure. This exercise is done by the departments in the light of the Annual Performance Plan (APP) fixed by the Corporate Office.

Submission of the budget proposals

After receiving the circular from co-ordinating agency, the departmental heads convene a meeting of all the concerning staff of the department and request them to submit their requirements for the budget year.

Discussion over the Proposals

After the submission of the requirements, they are thoroughly discussed and with necessary modification, a consolidated budget proposal of the department concerned is prepared. This proposal is forwarded to the cost and budget section for the purpose of co-ordination.

So far as the budget proposals of the operational departments are concerned, they are routed through the Production Planning Control & Sales Co-ordination Department for the purpose of giving them a composite shape in quantitative term. Thereafter the Cost and Budget Section translates them in to monetary terms. The Cost and Budget Section also co-ordinates various proposals for the purpose of discussion, modification and finalisation in the meetings of departmental heads with the Managing Director as chairperson.

Before translating the budget into the monetary term the Cost and Budget Section gives a thorough look upon the departmental budget proposals. Any anomaly, detected during the course of matching of the budget proposals, is pointed out and the department concerned is asked to submit a revised proposal after making necessary adjustments.

Thereafter by incorporating all these proposals, a comprehensive budget is shaped in a consolidated form to be put for finalization.

Finalisation of the Budget Proposals

A detailed discussion over the budget proposals is made in the light of production plan of Corporate Office before its finalisation. If it is felt that the budget proposals do not meet the targets of the Corporate Office, they are modified by the respective departments. Such revisions are made three to four times.

Thus, an extensive exercise is made before giving a final shape to the budget in Bokaro Steel Plant.

Approval

Once the budget is finalised, it is presented before the Board of Steel Authority of India Limited for its approval. The Managing Director of Bokaro Steel Plant alongwith the Executive Director (Works) and the General Manager (Finance & Accounts) presents the consolidated budget of the Plant before the Board. Thereafter, a detailed observation is made by the Board in the light of plans and policies of the Corporate Office. The Board asks the Bokaro Steel Plant management to modify the budget, if necessary. The budget is finalised by the Board of SAIL by the end of January, but the final approval is given only after the presentation of the Railway and Revenue budgets of the Central Government. In the light of the Railway and Revenue Budgets, necessary adjustments are made (if required) and then the budget is finally approved. This process is completed by the end of March of every year.

Allotment of Funds

When the budget is finally approved by the Board, the budgetary limit is frozen by the Corporate Office for the budget year. To the tune of the approved budgetary limit, funds are allocated by the SAIL to all its subsidiaries, likewise the allocation for Bokaro Steel Plant is also made. The Managing director of BSL is authorised to spend money under the limit through a delegated power. Within this limit, fund is allotted to all works and non-works departments at the plant level. For works departments, the fund for other expenditures is alloted by the Cost Control Department in the ratio of the approved budget for the concerning department. So far as non-works departments are concerned, the money for other expenditures is alloted by the Cost and Budget Section. The departmental allocation is made under different heads *i.e.* printing and stationery, Miscellaneous expenditures for routine work.

Budgeting for Planned Capital Expenditures

So far as the capital budgeting for planned capital expenditures is concerned, a complete budgetary exercise is followed in BSL. For commissioning units/projects under construction, proposals involve modifications in existing provisions as well as provisions not covered so far.

Capital investment proposals are initiated by the head of the department concerned in prescribed formats only after a thorough examination of the problems relating to existing provisions. Any proposal of up to Rs. 2 lakh is moved by a superintendent or assistant general manager of the beneficiary department, whereas the proposals of more than Rs. 2 lakh are initiated by the General Manager or Direct Reporting Officers (DROs) of the department concerned.

The beneficiary departments send their proposals for such capital expenditures to the Technical Investment Cell and Investment Planning Unit (TIC & IPU) to verify and judge the technical viability of the proposals. The superintendent of the TIC & IPU section, constitutes a survey committee for technical assistance, in co-ordination, with the GM/DROs of the departments concerned. The survey committee examines the proposal and sends it back to TIC & IPU with necessary recommendations and comments. Further, the TIC & IPU section sends these proposals (with the recommendations and comments of survey committee) to the capital expenditures committee (Agency constitutated for the purpose) for detailed observations and to obtain their comments on economics of the proposals. The committee consists of the members of Design Bureau, Finance Department, E D P, Maintenance, TIC & IPU Section and beneficiary departments. The committee considers the proposal from various angles, *i.e.,* investment worth, rate of return and pay back period etc., and makes specific recommendations based on its merit.

Thereafter the TIC and IPU Section sends it to the Capital Budgeting Section to give it a comprehensive shape. This Section presents the comprehensive capital budget proposal before the Managing Director through GM (Finance & Accounts) in coordination with concerning DROs for a final exercise. The proposals requiring the approval of the Board of SAIL are sent to the Corporate Office for their ultimate say.

Once the budget is approved by the Corporate Office, it is sent back to BSL for its implementation. Thereafter the sanction order is issued to the Design Bureau to prepare a detailed engineering drawing. Thus, the execution of the proposal starts in BSL. After implimentation, it is reviewed from time to time in the light of the factors considered at the time of its initiation and if needed it is revised with necessary adjustments.

5. Monitoring of the Budget

In Bokaro Steel Plant, the budget monitoring is done on a micro level. The actual results are compared with the budgeted amount on a month-wise, weekwise and even daywise basis.

The daily profitability statement is prepared by the Cost and Budget-Section and is presented before the Managing Director and the Executive Director (Works) by 10.00 AM of the following day. The most important thing that it includes, is the variance analysis. The deviation points are observed and the factors, responsible for such variances are highlighted. Thus, the specific points, that are affecting the daily profit adversely, are identified and corrective measures are taken at that very time to control further deviations.

In addition to the daily profit statement, a mid-month's report (MMR) and last month's report (LMR) are also prepared and sent to the Chairman, Steel Authority of India Limited through the Managing Director. The mid-month's report is sent on the

15th day of every month and the last months report is sent on the last day of the month. Both the reports consist of the figures of actual production techno-economic parameters and actual profit alongwith the budgeted output and profit. The cause of variance is also mentioned.

In the following month, the profit and loss account statement is prepared for the preceding month. In this statement, favourable and unfavourable factors are highlighted by the Cost and Budget Section. The Managing Director takes stock of the progress in meetings with the Direct Reporting Officers (DROs). Deviations are analysed and action plans are chalked out in the meetings. These action plans are circulated in all the concerning departments, units and shops. In the next meeting of the DROs it is reviewed as to how far the action plans are being implemented.

The Cost and Budget Section sends a monthly management information system (MIS) report also to the Director Finance (Corporate Office) through the General Manager (Finance & Accounts). Production and profitability are highlighted in this report. Thus, a micro level monitoring is made for the whole budgetary exercise by the Bokaro Steel Plant management in a well co-ordinated manner.

Budgetary Control in BSL

Budgetary control is the most important aspect of budgeting because set targets cannot be achieved in the absence of an effective control system over the important constituents of a budget. The budgetary control system in Bokaro Steel Plant can be observed by making a discussion over the control of some of its important constituents. They are :

Cost control and cost reduction

Analysis of cost variance

Inventory control

Consumption control

Sensitivity analysis

Techno-economic parameters.

Cost Control

For an effective cost control, both the standard cost and the actual cost sheets are prepared in BSL.

Based on the expenditures envisaged in the budget, the cost of production of each of the product, by-products, services, engineering shops and other related functionaries is ascertained. This cost is called standard cost of production. The standard cost, once prepared, remains unaltered throughout the year even though the prices or conditions, assumed in the budgeted standard cost, undergo changes. At the end of the year, after the closing of accounts, duly audited by the auditors, the annual cost statements are prepared for each of the major products, by products, services as well as engineering shops and overheads departments in BSL. Based on the annual cost statements, monthly cost reports are prepared to have an effective cost control. Alongwith these, cost variance reports are also prepared on a yearwise and monthwise basis.

The cost variances are calculated for the department as a whole as well as for each unit of each product. In addition to the monthly cost report, annual cost report and cost variances report, the following reports are also generated from out of the costing system being followed in the Plant :

(i) Daily profitability statement

(ii) Product profitability statement

(iii) Sensitivity analysis of important performance indicators immediately after the preparation of standard cost.

Thus, the cost control involves the following four major steps in BSL :

(a) Fixation of pre-determined standard/budget targets.

(b) Evaluation of actual performance.

(c) Comparison (of actual performance with pre-determined standards/budget/targets and analysis of variances.

(d) Taking a corrective measure in case of adverse variances.

The purpose of cost control is to achieve a certain pre-determined target through a continuous monitoring. It helps to control over-expenditures.

Cost Reduction

Cost reduction provides a solid base from which an additional profit can be realised. Innovation is a natural human urge. Cost reduction/cost effectiveness is an area where we can display our innovative skill. Budgets are utilised only as a control device for the purpose. A modest cost reduction programme can have a greater effect on profit than to solely increase sales.

In the emerging world of competitive business, only the achievement of set targets is not adequate. The process of cost reduction goes beyond cost control. The BSL has launched a massive drive for cost reduction at the plant level. The guiding principles adopted in the organisation in this regard are :

(a) Unit cost reduction by expenditure reduction in respect of a given volume of output.

(b) Unit cost reduction by increasing production *i.e.* increase in output, yield or rate of output for a given expenditure.

Qualities of Cost Reduction

(a) Cost reduction must be a "Real One" in the course of process or services rendered.

(b) Reduction must be a permanent one.

(c) Essential characteristics and the quality of products should be retained.

(d) The basic idea behind cost reduction is to provide a better way of doing everything.

Variance Analysis

The variance analysis is the analysis of cost which indicates the difference between the actual value and the standard value. A cost sheet provides all the basic data for the calculation of variances. In BSL variances are calculated for the following important aspects :

1. Cost Variance

Cost variance is an indicator of efficiency. It guides us for the areas where corrective actions are to be taken for an effective financial control of a process.

The cost variance is a difference between the standard and actual costs incurred during a period. When the actual cost is lower than the standard cost, the difference is known as — positive or favourable variance. The negative variance is called adverse. The following are the types of variances that can be computed for the variance analysis :

(a) Works cost variance
(b) Volume variance
(c) Expenditure variance
(d) Usage variance
(e) Rate variance
  (i) For input materials
  (ii) For fuel & services
(f) Credit variances for scraps, byproducts, rejections and wastages, etc.
(g) Other variances

2. Works Cost Variance

It is the difference between the standard works cost and the actual works cost.

3. Volume Variance

It is a part of the total variance which is due to an increase or decrease in the volume of production as compared to a budgeted output.

Volume Variance = Standard fixed cost for standard production – Standard fixed cost for actual production

Where standard fixed cost = operating, fixed cost + overheads.

4. Expenditure Variance

This is that portion of cost variance which is due to the difference between the standard expenditures for actual output and the actual expenditures incurred. The term expenditure consists of operating fixed cost and overheads. An adverse expenditure variance indicates that our expenditure in terms of the fixed cost is increasing

Expenditure variance = standard fixed cost for actual production — actual fixed cost for actual production.

5. Usage Variance

It is a part of the cost variance which is due to the difference between the standard usage and the actual usage of the inputs. A high input quality usually results in an adverse usage variance.

Usage variance = standard usage – actual usage

The main causes of usage variance are :

(a) Careless use of materials
(b) Change in quality or specification of products
(c) Inferior quality of purchase
(d) Inefficiency in production resulting in wastage
(e) Theft, leakage, shortage or evaporation
(f) Defective machines, tools, equipments, etc.
(g) Improper maintenance of machines etc. leading to breakdown and more usage
(h) Unrealistic standards or budget projections.

6. Rate Variance (Price Variance)

The variance due to the difference in the actual and the standard prices is known as rate variance.

Rate variance = budget rate–actual rate.

The main causes of price variances are :

(a) Change in basic purchase price of raw materials
(b) Use of substitute items having a higher or lower unit price

7. Credit Variance

While cost is incurred on input materials, credit is accrued on scrap, wastage, spoillage and by-product which can be sold or utilised in place of some other purchased input materials. The difference between the standard credit allowed for a standard output and an actual credit allowed for an actual output is known as credit variance.

8. Other Variances

Generally, this variance is minor in nature. Items of variances, which are not covered under the above variances, are considered as other variances. For example, variances on incentives, rewards, etc.

Sensitivity Analysis

The sensitivity analysis is a process to understand the impact of change in a performance level on cost and profitability. It is expressed in terms of a small unit to calculate the financial impact for a given level of production. For example, if B. F. coke rate in Blast Furnace is increased or decreased by one kg/t of hot metal, the calculation involved to work out the financial impact on the total annual production of H.M. will be termed as sensitivity analysis of B.F. coke rate. It helps the shop managers to determine suitable cost control/reduction measures so that the cost of production in their areas can be kept within the budgeted limit. Such an analysis is required to know the financial implications on the change in performance of techno economic parameters from their standard norms mainly.

Techno-Economic Variances

Techno-economic parameters related to each product are one of the major factors which have an impact on the production costs and overall profitability. Product yield, energy consumption, specific consumption of refractories, ingot mould and bottom plates are some of these parameters which have a considerable impact on the cost of different products. It is, therefore, necessary to analyse the techno-economic variances in financial terms on a weekly, monthly and yearly basis. This also helps in exercising a better control over the specific areas which give more adverse results.

Monitoring of Stores and Spares Consumption

Materials are the most important inputs for any production oriented organisation. It is the materials which are transformed into final products required for the fulfilment of desired human needs. Other business inputs like man, money and machines, have a supporting role for the transformation activity. In a process industry, like iron and steel, materials alone bear more than 60 per cent of the cost of production.

Steel plants require a huge amount of materials of various sizes, shapes, quality, quantity and other physical as well as chemical characteristics. These materials are grouped into the following categories :

(a) Capital equipment

(b) Raw materials

(c) Mechanical spares

(d) Electrical spares

(e) Refractories

(f) Conveyor belt

(g) Other consumables

The proper management of these materials plays an important role on the profitability performances of the organisation. Every rupee saved on materials gets reflected as a direct profit for the company. This envisages a high degree of co-ordination of all activities concerned with the management of materials right from the stage of material planning, procurement, scrutiny of specifications and drawings, ordering, receipt, inspection, payment, accountings, inventory control and consumption control.

Inventory Control

In BSL the process of inventory control consists of the following tools :

ABC analysis

XYZ analysis

VED analysis

ABC Analysis

It is a tool for the selective inventory control, carried out only once at the beginning of each financial year. In BSL, this analysis is made in terms of the value of annual consumption of each item. The items are categorized into AB & C with respect to their annual values as under :

Annual value of consumption	*Category*
Rs. 1 lac and above	A
Rs. 10,000 to Rs. 1 lac	B
Re. 1 to Rs. 10,000	C

XYZ Analysis

In BSL, the XYZ analysis is carried out on the basis of the stock at the end of the financial year

Annual value of stock	*Category*
Rs. 1 lac and above	A
Rs. 10,000 to Rs. 1 lac	B
Re. 1 to Rs. 10,000	C

VED Analysis

For an uninterrupted production process, it is essential to identify the materials as per their importance. For this the VED analysis is made in BSL. On the basis of the past experience, they are classified as Vital, Essential and Desirable items. It ensures a constant availability of vital and essential items.

Consumption Control

The inventory control can be effective only when there is a proper control over the consumption of materials. The consumption budget provides a base for control over the consumption of materials. In BSL, the budgetary provisions with regard to the consumption of various items are made available to all concerning departments for the purpose of control.

The actual consumption of each department for every month is computerised as per details available from EDP Centre and Stores Department. This is communicated to all departments for the control of a negative variation in consumption. In this regard, a system has been developed in BSL to provide department-wise and date-wise consumption details on the terminals of major departments connected through CMMS/EDP computers.

The items in stores, having no transaction for the last five years, are taken as dead stock and necessary action is taken for the closure of dead bin cards.

In BSL a regular monitoring of stores and spares is done with respect to the budgetary provisions to have an effective inventory control. The Managing Director also holds regular meetings for this purpose.

8

Summing-up

After having been freed from the long British rule, India had to struggle for the betterment of its destiny. The most crucial task before the first government of independent India was to get selfreliant in the field of business and industry. The political thinkers, who were at the helm of affairs at that time, chalked out a comprehensive plan to develop the country in all its facets under a mixed economic system. Accordingly, a number of public enterprises were established with massive investments as per the provisions of the industrial policy resolutions of 1948 and 1956, with a view to boosting the national economy through employment and resource generations.

The public sector performed almost upto the mark in regard to the employment generation but the country waited for a long time with great expectations regarding the most important task of resource generation, assigned to it.

If one goes into detail, one finds that the public sector has not been able to attain its objectives in its total perspective. The result is a well known fact. A big hue and cry began regarding its continuance on the same lines.

In the meantime, a new dawn of globalisation and liberalisation arose on the horizon of the world. It also brought in serious challenges before this sector. Now the government was not in favour to give them umbrella at all cost.

The declaration of the new industrial policy, 1991 was one of the most important steps taken by the government that brought about a fundamental change in the policies adopted earlier regarding this sector. The idea behind the present industrial policy was that it should not be given a tender lap of mother, *i.e.*, government. This idea may be corroborated by the following facts :

1. Previously core sector industries were mostly reserved for the public sector but now the restriction has been removed except a few like defence, atomic energy, etc.
2. Previously, huge provisions for subsidies were made available to the public sector undertakings through budget but now they have been reduced to a great extent.
3. Previously, a substantial allocation of funds was made through a budgetary support for public sector undertakings, now it has come to a negligible amount.
4. Previously, the policy of a heavy stress on and broad coverage of administered prices was adopted, now it has mostly been decontrolled.
5. Previously, the foreign investment was highly restricted, now it has been allowed with flexibility.
6. Previously, shares of public sector undertakings were held by the government, now the disinvestment policy has been adopted in this regard.
7. Previously, the market borrowings in regard to project financing were prohibited, now it has been allowed.
8. Previously, there was a provision of budgetary support for sick public sector undertakings, now it has been removed and the scheme of rehabilitation by Bureau of Industrial and Financial Reconstruction (BIFR) has been introduced.

In the light of the ongoing discussions regarding its very existence, privatisation and restructuring of this sector, efforts are being made to improve its functioning. Simultaneously, it has been signalled that the investment must be justified with appropriate returns. However, today the public sector is at cross roads.

The factors, responsible for the unsatisfactory performance of the public sector, may be enumerated as delay in project completion, cost over-run, under-utilisation of capacity, over-employment, lack of financial discipline, bureaucratic approach, undesired political interference, but the most important factor, that may be pointed out, is the lack of strict adherence to the profit planning and control in its true spirit.

At the initial stage of their establishment, there was a scant regard for adherence to budgeting-practices in public sector undertakings. In the meantime, the existing budgetary practices of public enterprises were subjected to extensive criticism by the Estimates Committee of the second Lok Sabha and the Committee on Public Undertakings. This condition remained almost the same till the setting-up of the Bureau of Public Enterprises (BPE). The government set-up the BPE in March, 1965 with an objective to give a desired dimension to the working of public enterprises. Prior to this, the Administrative Reforms Commission was already constituted to take stock of the working of this sector.

The Administrative Reforms Commission submitted its report in 1967. In its report, the commission amply emphasised the development of a sound budgetary system for the financial control and management of the public sector undertakings.

The Administrative Reforms Commission suggested that the public undertakings should prepare comprehensive budgets to embrace the entire organisation and to cover the entire aspects of all its functionaries *i.e.*, sales, production, production costs, manpower, township and welfare, research and development, capital expenditures, profit and loss, cash and capital employed. Further, it also suggested to apply a proper budgetary control system based on a performance evaluation system. "The comparison of performance data with budget estimates should be undertaken periodically, during the currency of the budget itself, so that the necessary corrective steps may be taken."[1] The public enterprises were also instructed to prepare business type budgets and to undertake a monthly review of sales, production and yield figures of each plant unit.

On the basis of the foregoing discussions of the budgeting-process in steel industry and other related industries of the public

1. Administrative Reforms Commission, *Report on Public Sector Undertakings*, 1967, p. 57.

sector, it is evident that the imagination of Estimates Committee, Committee on Public Undertakings, and the Administrative Reforms Commission has shown a considerable influence. The Bureau of Public Enterprises has issued all important guidelines to implement the recommendations of the committees and commission.

A comprehensive budgeting has been adopted in almost all the undertakings selected for the study but their adherence to it in its true spirit is yet to be implemented. Specially, the monitoring part of the budget is to be strengthened to give impetus to an effective performance so that the country with scarce resources may not be deprived of the expected returns on its investments. Simultaneously, a strong hand dealing is required with respect to the uncontrollable factors responsible, to a great extent, for such a staggering condition of the public sector.

APPENDIX

ANNEXURE-1

ORGANISATIONAL CHART (BSL)

ANNEXURE-II

IMPORTANT DATES OF COMMISSIONINGS IN BOKARO STEEL PLANT

UNIT	DATE OF COMMISSIONING
1	2
1. **Coke oven - By-Product Plant**	
Battery No. 1	29.03.1977
Battery No. 2	27.06.1976
Battery No. 3	18.10.1973
Battery No. 4	09.09.1972
Battery No. 5	29.07.1981
Battery No. 6	28.12.1982
Battery No. 7	23.02 1985
Battery No. 8	01.09.1993
Electrostatic Tar Precipitator No. 1	19.05.1977
Pyridine Recovery Unit	15.05.1978
Tar Distillation Plant	11.03.1980
Wash Oil Regeneration Unit	29.11.1979
Naptha Extraction Unit of TDP	23.04.1980
Benzol Rectification Plant	29.12.1986
Benzol Recovery and Distillation Unit	08.08.1987
Test Coke Oven Complex	16.04.1989
2. **Sulphuric Acid Plant**	
Unit No. 1	13.02.1978
Unit No. 2	25.01.1980
3. **Sintering Plant**	
Machine No. 1	19.09.1972
Machine No. 2	12.10.1977
Machine No. 3	15.06.1982

1	2
4. **Blast Furnace**	
Blast Furnace No. 1	03.10.1972
Blast Furnace No. 2	12.04.1976
Blast Furnace No. 3	26.02.1978
Blast Furnace No. 4	27.05.1981
Blast Furnace No. 5	09.06.1985
5. **Steel Melting Shop No. 1**	
Converter 'D'	31.01.1974
Converter 'C'	04.04.1974
Converter 'E'	27.04.1976
Converter 'B'	27.10.1977
Converter 'A'	30.12.1978
SCB Technology in Converter 'A'	18.02.1990
Steel Melting Shop No. 2	
Converter No. 1	03.06.1983
Converter No. 2	21.12.1984
Shop No. 2	01.01.1985
6. **Slabbing Mill**	
Slabbing Mill	30.12.1974
Soaking Pit No. 1	09.12.1974
Soaking Pit No. 2	11.03.1975
Soaking Pit No. 3	21.06.1976
Soaking Pit No. 4	11.10.1976
Soaking Pit No. 5	14.07.1980
Soaking Pit No. 6	04.11.1980
Soaking Pit No. 7	24.10.1981
Soaking Pit No. 8	19.11.1981
Soaking Pit No. 9	01.02.1985
Soaking Pit No. 10	01.02.1985
Soaking Pit No. 11	06.04.1989

1	2
Soaking Pit No. 12	22.09.1990
7. **Hot Strip Mill**	
Reheating Furnace No. 1	17.10.1975
Reheating Furnace No. 2	06.04.1978
Reheating Furnace No. 3	08.09.1984
Roughing Group	02.11.1975
Finishing Group	10.12.1975
Additional Coilyard	29.11.1986
8. **Hot Rolled Coil Finishing**	
Shearing Line No. 1	18.01.1976
Shearing Line No. 2	15.09.1976
Off Guage Shearing Line	31.05.1976
Silting Line	16.10.1976
9. **Cold Rolling Mills**	
4- Stand Tandam Mill	28.12-1976
5- Stand Tandom Mill	26.05.1989
Annealing Furnaces (1st & 2nd Groups)	02.06.1977
C.R.M. Complex	17.06.1977
Annealing Furnaces (3rd Group)	1981*
Annealing Furnaces (4th Group)	1982*
Annealing Furnaces (Exp. Stage)	30.06.1987
Skin Pass Mill (Exp. Stage)	11.05.1988
Hot Dip Galvanizing Line	18-02.1990
H.C.L. Regeneration Plant	12.05.1991
D.C.R. Mill	24.09.1991
10. **Cold Rolled Coil Finishing**	
Shearing Line No. 1	31.01.1978
Shearing Line No. 2	01.09.1977

*Dates not available.

1	2
Shearing Line No. 3	29.01. 1988
Slitting Line	06.12.1977
Slitting Line-II (Exp. Stage)	15.12.1988
Off Guage Shearing Line	27.04.1978
Amonia Cracking Line	22.07.1987
11. **Scrap and Salvage Department**	
Scrap Bursting Yard	18.06.78
Hydraulic Bailing Press	16.12.76
12. **R.M.P.**	
Kiln No. 1 (Dolomite)	
Kiln No. 2 (Lime)	10.12.1973
Kiln No. 3 (Lime)	25.06.1975
Kiln No. 4 (Lime)	22.12.1976
Kiln No. 5 (Lime)	26.04.1978
Kiln No. 6 (Lime)	11.02.1988
Kiln No. 7 (Lime)	29.12.1986
Brick Plant	08.04.1974
13. **Oxygen Plant**	
Asu No. 1	03.03.1976
Asu No. 2	02.12.1973
Asu No. 3	02.02.1978
Asu No. 4	05.07.1979
Asu No. 5	14.11.1988
Oxygen Filling Station	14.02.1972
Liquid Oxygen Tank	30.12.1986
Gaseous Oxygen Storage System	04.11.1987
14. **Acetylene Plant**	01.04.1972
15. **Nitrogen Argon Compressor Shop**	18.02.1990
16. **Auxiliary shops**	
Structural shop	27.12.1969

1	2
Machine Shop	17.09.1970
Forge Shop	17.6.1972
17. **Foundry**	
Non-Ferrous	01.12.1972
Cast Iron (Induction Furance)	05.07.1974
Ingot Mould (Bottom Plate Section)	23.05.1975
Ingot Mould (Ingot Mould Section)	27.09.1975
Steel Foundry	14.01.1975
18. **T.P.P.**	
Turbo Generator No. 1	26.12.1974
Turbo Generator No. 2	13.07.1972
Turbo Generator No. 3	30.10.1973
Boiler No. 1	17.04.1972
Boiler No. 2	23.08.1972
Boiler No. 3	06.06.1974
Boiler No. 4	27.06.1978
Boiler No. 5	23.06.1980
19. **C.P.P.**	
Boiler No. 6	14.11.1985
Boiler No. 7	30.07.1998
Boiler No. 8	19.02.1989
Turbo Generator No. 6	27.01.1986
Turbo Generator No. 7	16.09.1988
Turbo Generator No. 8	31.03.1989
20. **Slag Granulation Plant**	26.07.1979
21. **Oil Effluent Treatment Plant**	02.10.1991
22. **C.H. Slag Granulation in BF-5 (C.H.-10)**	29.12.95

Source : BSI., *Annual Statistics 1996-97.*

ANNEXURE III

TABLE

Capacity Utilisation in BSL

Products	Annual Capacity	1989-90 Ouptput (Tonnes)	1989-90 % of C.U.	1990-91 Output (Tonnes)	1990-91 % of C.U.
Hot Metal	4585000	3200144	70%	3267027	71%
Ingot Steel	4000000	2653846	66%	2806039	70%
Saleable Steel	3160000	2325175	74%	2426208	77%

Products	Annual Capacity	1991-92 Ouptput (Tonnes)	1991-92 % of C.U.	1992-93 Output (Tonnes)	1992-93 % of C.U.
Hot Metal	4585000	3673274	80%	3856111	84%
Ingot Steel	4000000	4417368	85%	3589424	90%
Saleable Steel	3160000	2730402	87%	2998501	95%

Products	Annual Capacity	1993-94 Ouptput (Tonnes)	1993-94 % of C.U.	1994-95 Output (Tonnes)	1994-95 % of C.U.
Hot Metal	4585000	4040011	88%	4090352	89%
Ingot Steel	4000000	3711650	93%	3655702	91%
Saleable Steel	3160000	3205192	102%	3168259	100%

Products	Annual Capacity	1995-96 Ouptput (Tonnes)	1995-96 % of C.U.	1996-97 Output (Tonnes)	1996-97 % of C.U.
Hot Metal	4585000	3968227	87%	4119293	90%
Ingot Steel	4000000	3680363	92%	3643746	91%
Saleable Steel	3160000	3329853	105%	3045805	96%

Source : *Annual Statistics*, BSL 1996-97, p. 3.

ANNEXURE-IV

List of Departments under Divisions

OPERATION DIVISION

(A) *Coke Oven and Bye-Product Plant*

(B) *Iron & Steel Zone :*

(i) Raw Materials and Material Handling Plant

(ii) Sintering Plant

(iii) Blast Furnace

(iv) Steel Melting Shop

(v) Scrap and Salvage

(vi) RMP & RED

(C) *Mill Zone*

(i) Slabbing Mill

(ii) Hot Strip Mill

(iii) H.R.C.F.

(iv) C.R.M.

(v) R.G.B.S.

(D) *Maintenance*

(i) Electrical

— C.P.E.'s Office

— Standardisation Cell (E)

— Power Plant

— Power Engg. Brigade

— D.M.W.

— Gas Utility and A.C.V.S.

— Intrumentation

— Tele Communication

— Electro Technical Laboratory

— Electrical Repair Shop

— Power Facilities Repair Shop

— Heavy Maintenance
— Water Supply
— Technical Bureau (E)

(ii) Mechanical

— Steel foundry and Pattern Shop
— Ingot Mould Foundry
— Cast Iron and Non-Ferrous Foundry
— Machine Shop
— Structural Shop
— Production Planning Shop
— Forge Shop
— Shop Maintenance
— Operational Garage
— Spare Parts Cell and I.D.Cell
— Standardisation (M)
— Heavy Maintenance (M)
— Capital Repair Shop
— Civil Engineering (Works)
— Technical Bureau (M)
— Import Substitution Cell
— Energy and Economy Department

(E) Safety Engineering Department

(F) Production Planning & Control and Sales Co-ordination

(G) Traffic

(H) Research & Development

PROJECT DIVISION

(i) Design Bureau

(ii) Mechanical Engineering

(iii) Electrical Engineering

(iv) Civil Engineering

(v) Equipment Planning Cell

(vi) P.M.C.
(vii) Quality Control & Service
(viii) Network Planning
(ix) Project Administration
(x) Modernisation Cont. Castings
(xi) Arch. and City Planning

SERVICE DIVISION

- — Managing Director's Office
- — Finance & Accounts
- — Aviation
- — Law Department
- — General Administration
- — Works Administration
- — Co-ordination
- — Personnel
- — Public Relation
- — Training & Management Development
- — Material Administration
- — Stores
- — Purchases
- — Education
- — Medical
- — Vigilance
- — Intelligence
- — E.D.P. Centre
- — Organisation & Method
- — Fire & Service
- — System Co-ordination
- — Sports & Civil Amenities
- — Security & Civil Defence
- — Spare Parts Cell (Mech.)

— Spare Parts Cell (Elec.)
— Long Range Planning
— Management Services Including TQP
— Land & Estate
— Hospitality
— Town Maintenance
— Peripheral Development
— Horticulture
— Public Health
— Industrial Engineering

ANNEXURE-V

Expenditures Incurred on Social Amenities (BSL)

Unit : Rs. in Crores

Head	1994-95	1995-96	1996-97	1997-98
Education	16.72	21.43	21.57	22.83
Township	48.97	59.04	53.59	55.35
Medical	25.87	28.71	27.26	26.56
Social/ Cultural Activities	01.96	02.19	02.12	02.24
Co-operative Societies	0.18	0.24	0.13	0.14
Transport & Dairy	03.53	04.22	04.40	04.83
Total	**97.23**	**115.83**	**109.07**	**111.95**

ANNEXURE-VI

Grade-wise Manpower Position in BSL (As on 31st March 1997)

Grades Executives Scale of Pay (Rs.)	Works	Admn.	Township	Project	Nos. Total	Grades Non-Executives Scale of Pay (Rs.)	Works	Admn.	Township	Project	Nos. Total
3700-7025 (EO)(JR Exec. T.)	8	-	-	-	8	2100-2660(S1)	865	52	152	6	1075
3700-7025 (EO)(Non Tr.)	4	6	5	-	15	2140-2791(S2)	1159	117	394	14	1684
4500-8250 (E1)(Mg. Tr.)	53	2	-	-	55	2190-29259(S3)	1761	156	357	9	2283
4500-8250(E1)	569	258	61	30	918	2245-3106(S4)	4843	455	799	31	6128
5650-9400(E2)	685	198	111	26	1020	2220-3432(SL1)	-	1	-	-	1
6600-9600(E3)	361	51	26	12	450	2310-3339(S5)	3054	425	776	216	4471
7500-9900(E4)	592	191	91	55	929	2390-3587(S6)	4128	121	393	61	4703
7950-10050(E5)	760	188	109	238	1295	2480-3959(S7)	6624	164	726	248	7782
8400-10200(E6)	227	82	25	97	431	2585-4132(S8)	4118	273	438	478	5307
9000-10500(E7)	50	12	3	14	79	2700-4429(S9)	1863	836	546	114	3359
9500-11500(E8)	8	5	2	6	21	3000-5028(S10)	1759	1634	707	73	4173
11500-13500(E9)	1	1	-	-	2	SOT/JOT	93	-	-	-	93
8500-9500 (Unrevised)	-	1	-	-	1	Casual	303	12	-	347	
Total	3318	995	433	478	5224	Total	30570	4246	5320	1250	41386

Source : BSL Statistics 1996-97.

WORKS CITED

Agrawal, R.C., *State Enterprises in India*, Chaitanya Publishing House, Allahabad, 1961.

Agrawal, J.D., *Capital Budgeting Decisions under Risk and Uncertainty*, Indian Institute of Finance, Delhi, 1988.

Anthony, Robert N. & David Young, *Management Control in Non Profit Organisations,* 4th Edition Homewood IL Irvin.

Bhatia, Sutinder, *Bokaro Steel Plant, Some Economic Aspects*, Bombay Popular Prakashan, 1991.

Bond, G.D., *Corporate Finance for Management.*

Brighans Eugene F & Ricks R. Bruce, *Reading in Essentials of Managerial Finance.*

Brimson J. Fraser R., *The Key Features of ABC Management Accounting* (U.K.).

Breton A. & T. Wintrobe, The Equilibrium size of Budget Maximising Bureau, *Journal of Political Economy*, Vol. 83, 1983.

Batty J., Corporate Planning and Budgetary Control Macdonald and Evans Ltd., 8 John Street, London, 1970.

Byrne, R.F.A. Charnes, W.W. Cooper, O.A. Devis and Dorothy Gilford, *Studies in Budgeting*, 1968.

Chambers, Reymondj, *Financial Management*, 1967.

Chopra, R.N., *Public Sector in India, Its Performance, Profitability and Industrial Relations*, Intellectual Publishing House, New Delhi, 1984.

Chakraborty, S.K., New Paradigm Management Accounting — Some distance views, Research Bulletin, *The Institute of Cost and Works Accountants of India*, January-July, 1992.

Chaubey, A.N., An unpublished thesis (accepted for the award of

Ph. D. Degree) on Budgeting in Public Sector Enterprises with special reference to CCL, Ranchi.

Charles T. Horgren, *Cost Accounting — A Managerial Emphasis*, Prentice Hall of India Pvt. Ltd., Delhi, 1976.

Das, S. Kumar, *The Economic History of India*, 1944.

Ernest, C. Miller, *Objectives and Standards : An Approach to Planning & Control*, A.M.A., Research Study (American Management Association), New York, 1966.

Gupta, K.R., *Issues in Public Enterprises*, S. Chand & Company, New Delhi, 1979.

Gadhok, D.N., *Accountability of Public Enterprises*, Sterling Publishers Pvt. Ltd., New Delhi, 81.

Gupta, R.K., *Public Enterprises in India*, Sahitya Bhawan, Agra, 1978.

Hanson, A.H., *Public Enterprises and Economic Development*, Routledge and Kegan Paul Ltd., London, 1965.

Horngren, C.T., Foster, G. (1987), *Cost Accounting : As Managerial Emphasis* (6th Edition) New Jersey, Prentice Hall.

Hill, Horace G. Jr., *Capital Expenditure Management*, Journal of Business, Vol. 28 (11955).

J. Mitchell, F., *Activity Based Costing, A Review with Case Studies*, London Chartered Institute of Management, 1990.

Joneyz J.W., *Material Burdening Management Accounting Can Support Competitive Strategy*, Management Accounting, 1987.

Jones, L.R. Fred Thompson & William, M. Zumeta , The "Logic of Budget Extension," *Economics of Education Review*, Vol. 6.

John, Sizer, *An Insight into the Management Accounting*, Richard Clay (The Chauser Press Ltd.), 1979.

Joel, Dean, *Top Management Policy on Plant Equipment & Product*, New York, Columbia University Press, 1962.

Jhon, G. Maclean, *How to Evaluate New Capital Investments*, Harward Business Review, 1958.

Kidwai, W.R. (1987), *The Threatening Storm Over Public Sector in India*, Standing Committee of Public Enterprises (SCOPE), New Delhi.

Keshava, G.P., *Readings in the Operational Problems of Public Enterprises*, Volume-I, S. Chand & Co., New Delhi, 1970.

Krishnamurty, V., Tryst with Steel, *Nehru and the Public Sector Steel Industry*, published by Intercorporate Marketing, New Delhi, 1988.

Khanna, K.K., *Management of Public Sector Enterprises in India*, Himalaya Publishing House, Bombay, 1988.

Khera, S.S., *Government in Business*, National Publishing House, New Delhi, 1977.

Koontz Herald & O Jonnel, Cyrill, *Principles of Management*, New York, Mc Graw Hill Book Co. 1955.

Keller J. Wayne & William L. Ferrara, *Management Accounting for Profit Control*, 1951.

Lotia, Chandrakant, *Management Problems of the Public Sector in India*, Manak Tala Bombay, 1967.

Laxmi Narain, *Principles of Practice of Public Enterprises Management*, S. Chand & Co., New Delhi, 1980.

Laxmi Narain, *Organisation Structure in Large Public Enterprises*, Ajanta Publication, Delhi, 1981.

Merit A.J. & Sykes Allen, *Capital Budgeting and Companies Finance*, Longrce Ltd., 1973.

Om Prakash, *Theory and Working of State Corporation with Special Reference to India*, George Allen & Unwin Ltd., London, 1962.

Pandey, I.M., *Financial Management*, Vikash Publishing House Pvt. Ltd., New Delhi, 1979.

Prem Chand, A., *Performance Budgeting*, Academic Books, Bombay, 1969.

Phyrr, A. Peter, *Zero Base Budgeting — A Practical Management Tool for Evaluation Expenses*, John Wiley and Sons, New York, 1973.

Prasad, N.K., *Principles and Practice of Cost Accounting*. 1977.

Russell, L. Ackoff, *A Concept of Corporate Planning*, John Willey & Sons, New York, 1970.

Rao, C.R. Ananda, *Public Enterprises and Parliamentary Committees in India*, 1982.

Shankariah, A., *Financial Management of Public Enterprises* (A Study of Budgeting in State Undertakings of Andhra Pradesh), 1983.

Sharma, T.R., *Working of State Enterprises in India.*

Scott, J.A., *Budgetary Control and Standard Costs*, Pitman Publishing, Toronto (Canada), 1970.

Singh, Ram Badan, *Economics of Public Sector Steel Industry in India,* Common Wealth Publisher, New Delhi, 1989.

Srinivasan, N.R., *The Corporate Story of SAIL*, published by Steel Authority of India Ltd., 1990.

Srinivasan, N.R., *The History of Bokaro*, published by the Steel Authority of India Ltd., 1988.

Verma, Austey, *The Economic Development of India*, 1941.

Welsch, Glenn A., *Budgeting : Profit Planning and Control*, Prentice Hall Pvt. Ltd., New Delhi, 1976.

Journals and Reports

Annual Statistics of BSL from 1988-89 to 1996-97.

Annual Reports of SAIL

Annual Reports of BSL from 1972-73 to 1996-97.

Annual Bokaro Magazine 1990-91 to 1996-97.

Administrative Reforms Commission Report on Public Sector Undertakings, 1967.

Bokaro News, published by Public Relations Department of Bokaro Steel Plant No. 1, 3 and 4 No. 7 (R), October 1994.

Choubey, R. N. (1986) — 'As the Heart Sees'... unpublished paper on Bokaro Steel Plant.

Dr. Hariharan, Background Paper on SAIL, Management Training Institute, Ranchi 1995.

Engineering New Frontiers — A Leaflet on MECON.

Five Year Plans

Growth, a monthly Journal of the Management Training Institute of SAIL, Ranchi from 1990-91 to 1996-97.

Government of India Resolution on Industrial Policy, 1948.

On Cost Effectiveness and Surplus Optimisation for Public sector Undertakings.

— Organised by the Department Of Public Enterprises, Government of India and the Institute of Cost and Works Accountants of India 1995.

The Management Accountant — Monthly Journal of the Institute of Cost and Works Accountants of India.

Government of India Resolution on Industrial Policy, 1956.

Government of India New Industrial Policy Resolution, July 1991.

Lok Udyog, July 1970 (Public Enterprises in Medieval India), a Monthly Journal of Bureau of Public Enterprises.

Mishra, R. K., Budgeting in Public Enterprises, published in *Management* in Govt. Journal of the Dept. of Personnel and Administrative Reforms, Vol. I, No. 4, January to March 1983.

Planning note on Bokaro Steel Project, Hindustan Steel Ltd., Ranchi, 3rd edition, 1963.

Public Enterprises Survey, a publication of Bureau of Public Enterprises from 1980-81 to 1993-94.

Report of the Estimates Committee, 2nd Lok Sabha.

Reports of the Committee on Public Undertakings, 3rd & 4th Lok Sabha.